MEMOIR OF A WHITE SHEEP

—

SURVIVING TRAUMA, DEPRESSION & ANXIETY

MY STORY

Ina Lackey

MEMOIR OF A WHITE SHEEP
SURVIVING TRAUMA, DEPRESSION & ANXIETY

BY

INA LACKEY

(an autobiography)

Publisher: Rise2Write Publishing LLC

ISBN: 979-8-9935526-2-0

www.rise2write.com

For information about custom editions, special sales, premium and bulk purchases, please contact: authorinalackey@gmail.com

THIS BOOK WAS NOT WRITTEN OR EDITED USING ANY FORM OF AI.

DEDICATION

This Memoir is dedicated to: God, for being my everything, and my three favorite men, my husband, Cary, and my sons, [Justin] and [Andrew] for their unwavering love and support. Love you, love you.

Thank you.

Ina/Mom ❤️

TABLE OF CONTENTS

INTRODUCTION

Thank you for taking this walk with me through my journey. It is my hope and prayer that this book will inspire you and those around you, who may be going through difficult times due to suicidal thoughts, mental illness, trauma, depression, anxiety, the current world affairs, and/or any other obstacle that may be preventing you from living a full and complete life.

It has taken me many years to find peace and joy, but I know that if I can do it, you can too. That is why I am sharing my story, because someone out there may need to hear this.

The names in this Memoir have been changed to protect the innocent and not-so-innocent that I either had the pleasure or misfortune to have in my life at one time or another.

I started this book a few times over the last year, but I could not quite get through reliving the most painful moments in my life, so I would quit writing, start again, and quit again. Only now do I believe that I have the courage to tell my story in the hope that it may help just one person and, if nothing else, I know that it was cathartic for me.

PART I: A Rough Start

T he summers were hot and humid, and snow covered the ground some winters -- my hometown of Lawton, Oklahoma is south of the historic Fort Sill military base, where I was born. The population then was just over 74,000 souls and the town was divided, both economically and racially, as many places in the Southwest and Midwest were. We did not live in the best neighborhood. The area was called "*Lawton View*" and was known to be a "*bad*" area.

Lawton was always a rough town, and maybe most military towns are, but Lawton View was more than just rough. It was notorious in the 70s and 80s for having a high crime rate, including violent crimes. Gangs, drugs, prostitution, sexual assaults, and armed robberies were prevalent, and I grew up in the middle of all of it.

The youngest of six children born to Mr. and Mrs. [Greene], I stood out like a sore thumb in the neighborhood. My older siblings were all brown-skinned, as were my mom and dad, but somehow, I was born with much lighter skin, which I grew to hate and despise. I occasionally would ask my family if I was adopted, but everyone would just say "*No*" and that black people came in all shades of brown, but I still felt different. I figured that I was adopted anyway and that I would find out the truth eventually.

The neighborhood and the schools that I attended back then, were predominantly black since the district that I lived in was mostly black back then. It quickly became apparent to me that my lighter skin complexion was going to be an issue and, wow, was I right.

I attended Will Rogers Elementary School. The walk was quite a hike from my home to school, but I made it by myself every day, that is until I started getting beat up on a regular basis by girls both at school and in my neighborhood. After coming home with so many black and blue marks, my mom asked a neighbor, an older boy named [Darnell], to walk me to school. He was helpful during that time, but he couldn't protect me forever. Imagine a little kid with a black eye. What could I have possibly done at such an early age to warrant such continued mental and physical abuse? The answer is absolutely nothing. Was it colorism? I was light-skinned, with long hair and many of them were...not. Was it self-hatred? Whatever the reason, those girls made my life a living hell while I lived in that town, and I could not wait to leave and get as far away as I could from them.

I was not "*black*" enough for them and so they bullied me constantly. I would have loved to have grown to be a sweet girl with a quiet, soft voice; dainty and girly with the opportunity to live without fear, but instead, I had to become tough to live in my neighborhood if I didn't want to get my butt kicked every day. I had to become street smart to survive, and that stays with you.

One year, a tornado destroyed our school in the middle of the night. It was a relief when we didn't have to go to school for awhile, at least until they put up a few trailers while the school was being rebuilt, but I dreaded going back. That was my first memory of wanting to commit suicide, because I always felt like there was no way out, and no one around me who understood.

An obvious question might be: *Didn't your siblings protect you?* Well, the older sibling, [Evelyn] [deceased] who was 16 years older than me, had joined the Air Force and was miles away, as was [Tom], the oldest son, who was away in the Army. [Laurence], the next oldest son, had also joined the Army. The youngest son, [David] [deceased] was also away in the Army. That left the sibling closest to my age (8 years older), [Nikki]. Nikki was still living at home as I was growing up and she knew about these constant fights but did nothing about it, in fact, every chance she had, she would either physically or mentally bully me too. I learned early on that even people who may live in the same house as you, the very people that you call "*family,*" could be as vicious as someone on the street, or more so. The fact is, I have had strangers in my life who were more like family to me than Nikki or Tom ever was.

David was my favorite sibling because he always tried to protect me, when he was around. One time, a neighbor was calling me "*half-breed,*" and David gave him a bloody nose, then he got a spanking from my dad. Ironically, you could say that he was the "*black sheep*" of the family.

As a child, I developed styes on my eyes and, unfortunately, sometimes they were present during school picture day. I hated those pictures! I looked like a neglected child being thrown away. My ponytails were always crooked, and I didn't look clean; a little girl, who no one seemed to care about. These styes were an indication of poor hygiene. Maybe it was because no one really cared for me, to make sure that my little face was nice and clean. I remember one time, going to the dentist and they said that I had a cavity; my dad was embarrassed and mad at me for not doing a better job of cleaning my teeth. It would have been great if someone had actually taught me the correct way to brush my teeth, but I was dealing with something more than just toothaches.

It was something unimaginable and something that changed me forever.

My dad, the only dad that I ever knew, was a hardworking man. Some called him Sergeant Green. He was in the Army and that is how we ended up in Lawton/Ft. Sill, Oklahoma. The other siblings had been born in different places, like Arkansas and Germany, and were the "*Army Brats*." By the time I was born, my parents had settled into retirement in Lawton. No-so-lucky me.

After retiring from the Army, my dad started working as a manager at a popular gymnasium on the Army base, so he was away from home a lot of the time. My dad was Superman. He not only worked to provide for the family financially; sometimes working two jobs, but he also cooked, cleaned, washed the dishes, did the laundry and everything else. My mom did not work. She was diagnosed in her early twenties as schizophrenic, and as far back as I can remember, I was either visiting her in some mental facility or watching her overly medicated, more like sedated, lying on the couch with only moments of lucidity. As she cycled in and out of her insanity, she dragged me with her. She told me that I was her favorite and she doted on me constantly, but her attachment to me was unhealthy and damaging, as you will see.

We all remember our first kiss, right? The boy or the girl's name, the place, and maybe even what they were wearing at the time. My first kiss was when my mom stuck her tongue deep into my mouth and attempted to tongue-kiss me. I was about four or five years old. I was confused and grossed out at the same time. I wish I did not have that memory stuck in my mind. It felt so unnatural, and I immediately pushed her away, and that was the start of being molested by my own mother, which lasted for at least four or five more years. So, as my life went on that way, I must have shifted into some kind of numb, survival mode.

I remember feeling so alone, with no one to talk to, no one to turn to, and nowhere to go. I became increasingly withdrawn; more and more depressed.

During those early years, my dad and I would go visit my mom at one of the mental institutions, either in town, or a few miles away, depending on the severity. I can vividly remember playing with paint by number sets in the visitation room and pretending like my life was normal, if just for a moment in time. Then, other months, when my mom came home, I knew that it was only a matter of time before she eventually would want me to sleep with her in her bed (my dad slept on the couch every night for years). When she was home, she would call out for me at night (I can still hear her voice yelling out my name ["*Kaaaaaaye*"] and it still haunts me). She would then help me up onto her tall bed. I would lay next to her, scared but I stayed very still and just focused on an object in the room, then she would start touching me, all over, making me touch her all over and then she would put my little body on top of hers, as she physically made me move up and down and press against her vagina while controlling my hips. She made me touch and grab her vagina and she touched mine. She moved my little hands across her breasts as she moaned in ecstasy. It felt so wrong and so strange, but I was paralyzed with fear and confusion. Sometimes, I would say *"No mommy, no"* and I would cry until she told me to stop.

I even recall one night, Nikki walked into my mom's bedroom and saw me on top of my mom, and she yelled, *"What are ya'll doing*!?" My mom quickly pushed me off her and pretended like nothing had happened but as I started to get older, I was sure that what she was doing to me was wrong and warped. I just didn't know how to make her stop doing it, but I desperately wanted her to stop. Sometimes, I hoped that she would just go back to the hospital.

I was scared all the time and didn't know what to do; should I tell someone, but tell who? She told me that it was our "*little secret*" because I was her favorite and she would always tell me that she was the only one who loved me and that no one else cared about me but her. I mean, most of the time, it felt that way, so I believed every word she said. I did not want the affection that my mom was giving to me, even though it was the only affection that I was receiving from anybody. I would lay awake in bed sometimes and just ask God, "*Why me?*"

The years went on that way. She was mostly subdued, and on the couch, and those were the times when I felt safest from being the target of her sexual fantasies, then something or someone would trigger her, and she would suddenly stop taking her medications. We would not actually see that she wasn't taking them, but it would become evident by her behavior, so everyone knew. However, the last thing anyone wanted to say was, "*Mom, are you taking your medicine?*" because she would absolutely fly into a rage.

Suddenly, she was no longer sitting on the couch watching her favorite TV shows and watching the world pass her by. She was feisty and sassy. She started fixing herself up again, doing her hair, painting her nails, wearing make-up and waist clenchers. She was trying to go out and do things, which all sounded great, but eventually, she would spiral into someone more extreme and beyond. She would spend tons of money on things that she didn't need, like more clothes, shoes, and purses, and she would start smoking cigarettes and drinking. She dragged me with her everywhere she went, and we would take taxis because by that stage, my dad would have taken away her car keys. We went to places on the military base. She would order her drink and order me a soda. I only remember her talking to people, but I don't remember who, or any of those details.

The one thing that I do remember is that I was the only kid sitting at the bar.

Towards the end of her worst insanity phases, she started doing some bizarre things, like going outside in the snow in her bikini and my dad's cowboy boots, taking her clothes off and dancing sexually (anywhere). One time, we went to the bank (she and I in the usual yellow taxi) and they would not give her any money, so she made me sit on the floor with her in the middle of the bank while she protested, stating that she had millions in that bank, and they were refusing to give it to her. I was constantly humiliated and embarrassed by her in some way or another. She loved a song called *"Please Don't Go"* and she always made me sing it, both in public and private. People would just stare in shock. I wanted to crawl in a hole and die.

Then, at some point, she would become so manic that it was dangerous to be around her. Sometimes I would hide in the closet and stack blankets and stuff over me. I hate recalling these memories – *deep breath* – she and my dad would argue and fight, sometimes physically. I just covered my ears when they fought. I am not sure why he wouldn't call someone right away when it got bad, but instead, sometimes, he chose to tie her up and limit her to one room of the house that had a bathroom. It was an add-on to the house (*"the den"*), so it was separated from the rest of the house by just a sliding glass door that would have previously exited into the backyard. Depending on how violent she would get, sometimes, my dad would even hog tie her and keep her that way for hours, but when she calmed down, he would then untie her. Her behavior was often unpredictable, so there was always this constant tension in the home during those times. I never felt safe or sure of anything.

I have a memory in my head that I pray goes away one day.

On this day, she was locked in the den again but untied. I was talking to her through the glass door, and she seemed calm at that time and asked my dad for a drink of water. The details are fuzzy, but I remember him not getting her the water fast enough and she did something unthinkable as a result. This part is crystal clear, unfortunately. She urinated in a cup and drank it! Years later, I asked my dad about that incident, and he was shocked that I remembered. I told Nikki about it, but she didn't believe me, that is until she got a job at the courthouse years later and read about it in the court files.

Eventually, my mom would become so out of control that my dad would finally call 911 and men would come dressed in all white and take her back to the mental hospital. It would take about three or four of them to get her into a straitjacket because she was fighting the whole time. She had this incredible will and strength that even the hospital workers would comment on. Then, days and sometimes weeks would pass by until we could see or talk to her again, but when it was time to visit, she was clearly overly medicated, slow-moving, slow-talking, and barely there. I think it was a combination of the electric shock treatments they gave her and the medications, but it was a terrible thing to experience. No child should ever see anyone after they have had a shock treatment. She was drooling, incoherent, and downright scary looking with her hair sticking up. I had nightmares about that for years. She would come home and there she sat on the couch and the cycle continued that way like clockwork for many years.

I think I liked her best when she finally stabilized. She was nice and sweet. A caring and nurturing mother. The kind of mother that I loved and needed, but that phase just never lasted long enough. It was like constantly saying hello and goodbye to the same person over and over again.

One of these occasions is etched in my memory. I was about eight years old at the time and my mom had gone off the rails again.

My dad called 911 and the men in white barged into my mom's bedroom and they were trying to get her into a straitjacket when my dad yelled at me to get out of the way and that's when I learned the truth. My mom yelled out, *"Get your hands off her! She's not your daughter!"*

5-Year-Old Me
Lawton, Oklahoma

Chapter One: The White Sheep

The room seemed to close in on me. My ears started to ring, I couldn't see, I couldn't think, and I couldn't breathe. I had just learned that my dad was not my *"real"* dad, so eventually, I asked him about what my mom had just said but his response was his usual response whenever I asked him what was wrong with her, he would just say, *"Your mama is sick."*

My mom's words haunted me for months and I felt more alone than I ever had before. I cried myself to sleep so many nights that I would wake up with a red face, and eyes almost swollen shut. I continued to go to school, and my dad would fix my hair when my mom was not around. I was still getting beat up by the neighborhood bullies, and in those days, I did not fight back, so the days were long, and the nights were even longer.

Living in a neighborhood like I did, I was constantly shocked by one thing or another, like walking to school one day and seeing my first dead body. The path that I would take to school took me through a park located behind my house. Then, I had to walk across several other residential streets and one main busy street before reaching school. So, on this particular day, I was walking through the park alone, and I heard all the dogs barking (they were in most back yards for protection), but then I heard two men arguing and a woman shouting, their voices got louder as I got closer, and then I heard a loud pop! I looked to my right and one of the men had shot the other man in the head. The woman was screaming. As he fell to the ground, I heard his head hit the concrete and saw the blood flowing. I took off running and could hardly catch my breath by the time I reached the donut shop close to my school. I had nightmares about that for years, too.

When my mom returned home from her most recent trip to the state mental hospital, I was full of questions, and here is the story she told me:

> My dad had been stationed in many different places, and she had apparently found pictures of him with other women in his Army duffel bag. She believed that because she gave him a hard time about cheating, he called her "*crazy*" and that he purposely put her into mental institutions for years, so that he could carry on his affairs without her knowledge. She told me that she said to him, "*I'm going to have a pretty little girl one day and she's not going to be your daughter.*" She said that he had previously been stationed in Vietnam, but she and their five children stayed behind. She said that he stopped sending money home, so she started going to the NCO Club on the military base. One night, she and her friend met a man there, who she called "*True Blue.*" He was white, tall, with brown hair and blue eyes. She told me his first and last name and that they loved each other. She said that when she was six months pregnant with me, that my dad returned home from Vietnam and wanted to work things out but with a few conditions: that she end the affair immediately, that she never tell him about me, never see him again, and never tell anyone else.

I have no doubt that my dad had affairs, but she *did* have a mental illness that no doubt contributed to her paranoia. In any case, I was too young to understand all of that but what I clearly understood was that I had two parents that didn't feel like parents to me at all, and I became curious about this "*white man.*" That's how Nikki referred to him when she would yell at me to stop talking about him.

I used to fantasize about meeting him often. There was a piece of the puzzle that just wasn't there and that made it hard for me to feel that connection with my family. It was part of the *"Midwest Code"* that you did not talk about family business, especially ours, so eventually, I stopped bringing him up.

Later in my life, my older sister, Evelyn told me that she met my biological father during that time. She said that she came home from school one day to find him sitting in the living room and that she asked him if he knew her father, to which he replied *"No,"* she then walked off, refusing to shake his hand. That was my sister Evelyn.

Fast forward, I was about 9 years old at this point and I am sure that my mother was beyond exhausted, so sometimes she would tell Nikki to take me with her when she went out with her friends, and begrudgingly, Nikki did, but she would push me around the whole time; hitting me, pushing me down, and pulling my hair. Finally, when my mom would say, *"Take her with you."* I would scream *"Noooo!"* while holding onto the back of my mom's leg for dear life! It was also during this time that I began to resist my mom's advances when she reached that phase. I was getting older and building up resentment. I was feeling less frail and more determined to know why all of this was happening to *me*, and I did not like the fact that they had lied to me for years. I lost trust in everything and everyone.

I tried to make friends the best I could, but I think I was too socially awkward, not necessarily shy, but extremely guarded and never really knowing what to say or do. I did not want to get too close to anyone and have them learn my dirty secret. I felt strange and unfamiliar, especially in groups.

I remember one friend coming over to my house and after meeting my mom, she asked, *"Is your mom slow?"* After that, I was hesitant to invite anyone over to my house.

It was hard to make friends because I felt so dirty and damaged. I'm sure you've heard this before from biracial or multiracial people, that I was too *"white-looking"* for black people and *"too black"* for white people, especially in Oklahoma where they didn't hide their distaste for you.

So, I really did not fit in with anyone in my own house or outside my house, and the feeling of hopelessness seemed to loom over me daily. It was a constant feeling that something was just *"off"* inside and there were never any calm thoughts; just racing emotions. I used to write on the wall in my bedroom, behind my dresser and mostly it was venting about my daily frustrations and my mom. I never even had a birthday party as a child, and maybe that's why no matter how old I get, I *"do it big"* for my birthday every year. I take the day off from work and I celebrate all week.

You see, I was alone most of the time and hardly left the house. There was no family time or eating at the table (not even once) and we never went out to eat (not even once). We did not have any other family in Lawton, so my *"support system"* existed in this cloudy bubble.

We did manage to take occasional trips to Texas to visit extended family. Mostly, we would go for family reunions and, of course, I felt like an outsider there too and treated like one by some family members. Despite being the only light-skinned person there, I jumped right in and tried to connect and met some wonderful aunts, uncles and cousins. We would stop in Houston to visit my dad's family and then to Ft. Worth to visit my mom's family.

My dad's father was deceased, and his mother clearly knew that I was not his child, so she was distant from me - not mean - just indifferent. Both my mom's mother and father were also deceased, so I never experienced having loving grandparents, like many people do.

On one of the earlier trips to Texas when I was at my mom's family reunion, I noticed an uncle, [Uncle Lee], and many of the family members were ignoring him, just as some did me. He came up to me and said, "*hey Kaye, whatcha know good?*" He was nice and friendly, and treated me like a special niece. He looked a lot like my mom too. Then later, one of the cousins told me why she and others were afraid of him and didn't talk to him that much (I almost left this part out of the book on purpose because it is both embarrassing and horrific, but it does give some context related to inherited traits, such as mental illness).

> The story goes, that my Uncle Lee had mental problems for years and the family tried to get him help, but his condition progressively worsened. On this particular day in 1971, he had a complete mental breakdown and murdered every family member in the house, including a brother, a sister, a cousin and their mother. Their father died days later from his gunshot wound. I was two years old when it happened.

So, going through life, knowing that deep dark family secret only prepared me for what I expected would be my demise in some way or another. I lived so many years expecting to grow up and become my mother, or something like her, and I dreaded that day arriving.

As I look back now, sometimes, it is hard for me to remember certain periods of my life because I spent so many years trying to block them out of my memories. I came to realize that those early formative years shaped and molded me into the woman that I am today, and that if I don't attempt to remember and try to understand those memories, it may be harder to work through the pain -- the same pain that has hindered my ability to heal and grow for so long, as I lived most of my days stuck in a dark cloud of despair.

Mama and Daddy

Chapter Two: Attempt No. 1

The first time I tried to commit suicide, I was around 11 years old.

My mom called out to me one evening, wanting my company, and I felt sick to my stomach at the thought of another night doing this awful thing with her. I did not want her to touch me in any way, and she started to sense that, but for some reason, this night, I had the courage and physical strength to squirm away from her. She was surprised, but more than that, she was hurt and even angry that I rejected her. Her advances became less and less after that, but the damage was already done.

After that, I really felt unloved, unlovable, and lonely. I believed that I only had one or two friends that were nice to me, but I did not dare invite them to my house. I still felt weird around other people, especially when people stared at me, because I felt that they must know what happened to me, and I was ashamed of it.

I had little to no supervision for most of my upbringing, so with a dad working constantly and a mom, who was rarely present, mentally, or physically, I pretty much went unnoticed. That is, when Nikki and I weren't arguing.

One time, they were looking at family photo albums and Nikki saw a baby picture of me and said, *"look, that's when Kaye was a little boy - haha."* I yelled out something like, *"No, I wasn't!"* and that opened the door to the *"queen of insults,"* who went on to say something to the effect of, *I didn't belong there anyway, so why don't I just leave?*

I packed my bags and said that I was running away and that's when Nikki started to run around the house singing, "*Hit the roooad Jack and don't ya come back no more, no more, no more, no more…* ♪…" I went walking around the neighborhood until it got dark, but then I got scared and went home. It was around that same time that I took a bunch of pills that someone had given me for headaches, which I often had. They were small and pink, and we called them "*baby pills*" and I took all of them in the bottle, then I laid down in my bed and went to sleep, ready to say good-bye to this whole nightmare of a world and everyone in it.

Early the next morning, my eyes opened, and I immediately began to throw up. I was nauseous all day, my stomach hurt, and I was so disappointed that I was still stuck in this family and stuck in this life. I stayed home from school that day, and no one was the wiser. I'm not sure anyone really cared, but I knew then that it would not be my last time trying to escape this world. I just had to figure out a better way.

PART II: Living with the Pain

I got used to feeling empty inside and numb to the pain. Nothing had really changed, except that my mom had finally stopped molesting me. I was just existing in this bizarre world where I felt like I was on my own, living in a house with strangers. One time, I asked my dad why he never told me that he loved me, and he said something to the effect that *he buys the food, pays the bills, etc. and that was his way of showing that he cared*. I guess I couldn't expect much more than that. After all, it takes a special kind of man to raise another man's child and every day that he looked at me, it must have reminded him of the affair, so I never asked him that question again.

During this time, my mom was going to the hospital less and less. They must have found the right combination of medicines because she seemed to stabilize somewhat for a few years, although she never developed any interest in doing anything other than watching TV. I believe she was depressed and probably resigned to spending the rest of her days and nights in the house and in front of the TV, with the *TV Guide* in hand, and watching her favorite shows. She did not interact with anyone outside of the home, other than occasionally with her sisters in Texas. The neighborhood dubbed her "*the Crazy Lady*" for all the times they saw a police car or an ambulance at our house as they watched on the sidelines in horror. I remember the look on their faces. They seemed to pity me. I guess I learned to pity myself.

At some point, someone, and I don't remember who, took me to church. I think it was my mom but when I close my eyes and picture myself in church when I was little, I am standing there alone, and the one memory that is crystal clear is learning about God and how He is always with us. It always felt good to go to church, like going to the hospital when you're sick. I always felt better when I was there.

I even remember getting baptized. I felt protected. My mother was a religious woman, despite her challenges. She taught me the 23rd Psalm and told me to recite it anytime I felt afraid. That one scripture has helped me greatly throughout my life.

I am sure that God was with me every step of the way and that He helped me to survive and live through all the pain. I wanted to be happy. I wanted to smile, with smiling eyes. I wanted to see Jesus one day and I wanted so badly to believe that one day, things would get better for me. I just didn't know that it would take so long.

I learned to live with pain by learning how to protect myself against it and making sure that no one would ever hurt me again. That was the beginning of building up an indestructible wall.

Chapter Three: From Sadness to Rage

At the start of middle school, I was about 12 years old. I went to Central Junior High School, which was a lot bigger than my old elementary school and the problems that I had with girls also got a lot bigger. There was one family of about five sisters [the Beavers], who I did not know in elementary school, but I became their target for the next few school years. They literally hated me for no reason at all and took every opportunity they had to spew every ounce of their anger directly towards me.

After being pushed around and embarrassed for so many years, I started to fight back, and the fights often resulted in suspension from school. I wouldn't even get in trouble at home because when I told my mom that kids at school hit me, she would say *"Hit them back!"* and when I told her that they were calling me names, she just said, *"Call them names back!"* Three days here, and three days there, the suspensions continued. I was fighting all of the time. Sometimes, I would win and other times, I would lose, but no matter how big they were, I always fought back until someone broke it up.

I remember how sore I would be the next day after a fight. My arms and legs were sore, with scratches and bruises everywhere, but after some time, I learned to protect myself better and if they got too close to me, I was the one who threw the first punch, attempting to knock them out. I literally could not go anywhere without girls starting fights with me. The mall, the arcade, or just walking to the corner store to buy candy. They would call me *"White Girl,"* *"Half-Breed,"* *"White Bitch,"* *"Yellow Bitch,"* *"Red Bitch,"* and *"Mulatto Bitch."* They would say that I thought that I was cute and better than them. It became easier to stay at home and fake an illness than to go to school. I didn't care much about my meager social life.

I didn't belong to any clubs or play any sports. I just tried to make it through each day without conflict.

One of the worst fights I had was when a girl named [Pumpkin] wanted to fight me. She lived in another neighborhood across the tracks and so she took a different school bus from school that particular day. The rumors were circulating that she wanted to fight me, of course, for no apparent reason, but the word got back to me and so, I was on high alert.

That morning, I grabbed a steak knife from the kitchen on my way out the door and went about my day looking behind my back the whole time. She only gave me dirty looks during the day but, when school ended, she got on *my* bus to go to *my* neighborhood instead of *her* own, and it was then that I knew that day would be the day that I had to fight her.

The school bus reached 12th street and Georgia, and I stepped off the bus carefully as I looked from side to side. She got off the bus right behind me and called my name. I guess I could have walked away and ignored her, but she probably would have attacked me from behind. I certainly was not going to run from Pumpkin, so she started talking trash, asking me about something she heard I said, she then started calling my mom *"crazy"* and saying that I was crazy just like her. My blood was boiling, and I really did want to avoid fighting her but before I knew it, I turned around and she hit me in the face. We started fighting and I could tell that she was stronger than me and so I pulled the knife out and when she reached to hit me again, I grabbed her and sliced down her arm. It was so deep that I could see the white layer underneath her skin. She was screaming and blood was everywhere. She ran across the street to a neighbor's house, and they let her inside. I remember being so angry that I chased after her with the knife.

When I reached their front door, I could see her holding her arm under their kitchen faucet and I began cutting through the screen door trying to get at her. It took a couple of people, and a long time for me to calm down. I saw red and I wanted to hurt her badly.

It was hard for me to concentrate on schoolwork when I was dealing with so many self-doubting thoughts that raced through my mind. Ironically, I was still somehow able to do well in school despite all the fighting. I always had A's and B's on my report card (except for a C in math) and I was proud of myself for at least that much, but when I came home and proudly showed my report card to whoever would pay attention to me that day, they would just place it on top of our fake fireplace and spill juice on it eventually. I had to learn how to motivate myself.

Consequently, those were my adolescent years, and with everything that I had to deal with, now people really saw me as some type of freak, especially after the incident with Pumpkin. I was confirmed as "*crazy.*" It was hard to keep friends, and even though it was not as hard to have a boyfriend, most boys found that my reputation preceded me. Who wants a girlfriend who knows how to kick somebody's ass? Especially when I cut my hair short to make it harder for girls to pull.

I found myself becoming more and more angry and resentful. Angry, because I felt that I had done nothing to warrant the bullying, the torments, and the ridicule. I was angry because I felt alone and scared all of the time. I was angry because I didn't receive love, nurturing, and care that every child needs to feel safe. I felt resentment towards my mother because of what she had done to me because it seemed to cripple me socially. I hated that I felt different from other people, no matter what race. I started to hate *me*.

23

I could feel myself spiraling out of control because I kept thinking about suicide and how leaving this earth would put me out of my misery. The hole in my heart felt bottomless, and I just could not see any other way out.

Chapter Four: Attempt No. 2

The second time I tried to commit suicide, I made it look like an accident, but I only ended up with lifelong back and hip problems for my trouble. I was 14 years old.

The fighting had subsided somewhat, but I had gained a reputation for being *"crazy"* like my mom. They even gave me the nickname *"Zorro,"* but I was not proud of what I had done. I did not want that type of notoriety. I just wanted to be left alone but I guess that was too much to ask.

I made a couple of friends during that time. There was one night when I was at a popular fast-food restaurant, and three or four girls tried to jump me and a girl from my neighborhood was there, who was older and bigger, and she came to my defense. Her name was [Niecy]. She had dark, beautiful skin, a pretty face, shapely figure, and she was a wonderful person. She and I became good friends, but I didn't visit her much because she lived in *the* very worst part of Lawton View and her mom was a prostitute. When I would go to her house in the projects, I would see men come and go and I didn't like the way they looked at me, so I didn't go to her house much. I finally invited her to my house, and I braced myself for the questions, but she never said a word about my mom.

She talked about sex a lot and I was getting curious… and aroused. Was *she* getting me aroused or was it hearing all of the sexual content? I didn't know, and it scared me. Did my mom make me gay? I wanted to prove to myself that I wasn't a lesbian, so I lost my virginity earlier than I should have. I wish I had a *me* back then to reassure me that I was enough, to value myself and not feel like a dirty mistake. I was only 14 years old, and he was 18 years old. I was feeling sexual and desirable.

All the boys my age were way too immature for me, but this guy only wanted to use me. Of course, I didn't know that at the time. It only confirmed to me that no one really cares and that if you're nice, people take your kindness for weakness and plot to use you for whatever they can. Around this time, I finally found a friend who I could kind of trust. Her name is [Mimi] and we are still good friends to this day. She lived in a nice part of town. We went to different schools. Her parents were educators. I first met Mimi at an ice cream parlor where she worked. When she asked me my name and I told her, she said, "*I know you, and you are too cute to be fighting.*" We hit it off from the beginning, but her parents were strict, and she could not socialize with anyone who lived in Lawton View, especially me. Mimi was popular. She was homecoming queen; cheerleader and she played sports. She was active in the church, and everyone loved her, and I know that her parents only wanted the best for her by keeping her away from someone they thought might be a bad influence. Her cousin was my first boyfriend. He even gave me my first promise ring, but I threw it at him when he came over to my house with hickeys.

That break up did not impact me too much, but I did learn to truly keep my feelings to myself and not get too close to anyone. It was easy for me to be a loner because that was the only thing that felt normal.

Then one day, a girl from my neighborhood asked me if I wanted to walk with her to a nearby neighborhood called Ranch Oak. We just hung out at the park there but when it started to turn dark, we headed back home, and her cousin walked with us. We reached 11th Street, a busy road with the airport just a couple of miles down the street and I remember that we started to run as it got darker. I reached 11th Street first and had stopped to look back to see where they were. When I turned around, I saw a car coming fast and then that's when it occurred to me.

If I just stood there, that car would surely hit and kill me instantly because it was going too fast, so I closed my eyes and braced myself for the impact. Bam! The next thing I remember, I was flying into the air and landed in a nearby ditch, near a metal fence. After that, the next thing I remember was being in the hospital lying on the cold metal of an x-ray table. I had broken my right pelvic bone in two places, had a concussion, with bruises and scratches all over. The driver was estimated to be going approximately 50 mph, and she never stopped -- another failed suicide attempt. Damn.

Chapter Five: The Struggle Continues

The next year or so involved recovery from the car accident. They took me to the same hospital on the military base where I was born. They did not operate on me or put any type of brace on my hip. I just laid there for months as the bone healed and grew back on its own and it grew back tilted to the right. Just my luck.

After I was finally able to move around, I was in a wheelchair for months and then finally on crutches for what seemed like an eternity. I literally had to learn how to walk all over again. I got behind in school but, fortunately, was able to catch up. At least this gave me a reprieve from the mean girls.

I was in the 10th grade when I had my last fight at school. I was all healed up, back in school full-time, and dating one of the best high school basketball players at that time. His name was [Parker] but they nicknamed him "*MJ*" due to his skills on the court. One night, he was at my house, and we were just watching TV when my mom walked into the family room. She looked at him, looked at me and said, "*Kaye, did you take your P.I.L.L.?*" I had started taking birth control, and she really asked me in front of him if I had taken my birth control pill, attempting to be discreet by spelling the word, not realizing that he was old enough to spell too! I just played it off with a laugh and said, "*Yeah, mom.*"

Parker was cool until his side chick let me know that they were still messing around and I invited her over to confront him together. He was so mad at her for telling me about them that he picked her up and threw her to the ground, breaking her arm. Two people can't be crazy in a relationship, so I ran for cover after that. It was later rumored that when I started dating my new boyfriend, Parker slit the tires of that guy's Ford Mustang GT.

I tried to go on and mind my business, but the bullying never really stopped. Even if I wasn't being physically pushed around as I had before, I was still being tormented in other ways: like having toilet paper draped all over my front yard and trees, like egging my house and cars, like me walking down the hallway in school (the breezeway) and being yanked from behind by someone pulling my ponytail or shirt but no one claimed to have done it when I turned around. That same anger and rage that I allowed to fester within me was rearing its ugly head. I just wanted to be left alone. I tried to ignore the girls, but it seemed to me that they were bound and determined to hate and hurt me. When I tried to be nice to them, my kindness was never received and my aloofness was perceived as being stuck up, but I was simply an introvert, or at least, I was safer being an introvert.

It came to a point where about three different other sisters were planning to gang up on me. These girls also lived in Lawton View and were just two streets away from me. They were rumored to have a plan to cut my face with a razorblade, and to burn my hair with a lighter. For weeks, I was looking over my shoulder just waiting for them to strike, and then it happened.

It was the first thing in the morning, at Lawton Senior High School. I was walking to my first-hour class, when the larger of the sisters, [Butch] jumped out from around a corner and stabbed me in the face with a metal fingernail file and blood started squirting out of my face. I was furiously fighting back and barely noticed the blood that covered my face and shirt. Then, another sister jumped in and knocked me to the ground, and that's when I saw something shiny on the floor. It was a paint scraper. I quickly picked it up, swung and cut Butch across her forehead. They all then ran to the bathroom. I was hauled away to the principal's office and was kept there until the police arrived. The police promptly took me to jail.

I stayed in jail for one night and got expelled from my high school indefinitely. My mom was worried, and my dad was upset with me. He was mad because my actions had caused him some problems, including having to hire an attorney to represent me in the court case. Ultimately, there was a settlement reached. My dad had to pay Butch's medical bills, and after reviewing my history, the judge sentenced me to 6 months out of the State of Oklahoma. My older brother, Tom and his wife [Trudy] allowed me to stay with them in Florida, but that did not work out too well either.

I moved to Clearwater, Florida at 15 years old. At first, it was okay. Tom taught me some Hapkido moves, and I enjoyed getting to know my two nephews better. It was too late for me to start school in their district to try and make up some time, so I started my first job at Burger King. Trudy and I didn't connect well but I was a good house guest. I helped with the cooking and cleaning, watched my nephews, and anything else they asked me to do. I enjoyed making my own money, the Florida weather was beautiful, and I liked being far away from Lawton View.

I was there for about 4 months when one day, Trudy came home from work with a big bouquet of red roses, and I heard her on the phone with someone who I believed to be a man. She thanked him for the flowers and their muffled conversation continued. After Tom got home from work, I told him about the flowers and the call. At first, he didn't believe me, and she was furious that I told him. They argued for days, then finally, she told him that either I go, or she goes. I was back in Lawton View the same week and had to stay in the house for the next 2 months to avoid violating the judge's order.

There were three high schools in Lawton at that time, and the next school year, I had to enroll in a different high school from the one I'd been kicked out of permanently. It was nice, clean, and their books were not torn apart.

It was also located in a good neighborhood with a mix of students, but they were mostly white. My reputation had preceded me there too, so on day one, I was called into the principal's office where they gave me a lecture and a warning about what they would not tolerate at their school. I felt like I was starting off on the wrong foot, so I didn't even bother trying to be nice or make friends. I just did my work and left. I did well in that high school, and ultimately graduated from it, but I also hated it because it was the first time that I experienced discrimination (from whites). It was just a difference in the way that whites spoke to non-whites, treated non-whites, and handled situations with preferential treatment of whites. Sometimes subtle, and other times not so subtle.

I got a part-time job at a fast-food drive-in down the street from my new high school, but when I slipped on the winter ice in my roller skates, I decided to quit rather than risk more damage to my hip. I knew that I had to do something, because my dad made it clear that I had to move out at age 18, but when I applied for college and needed his financial information for the application, he told me that it was *"none of their damn business how much he made!"* He said if I wanted someone to pay for my college, then I should join the military, like everybody else.

My next job was in a men's clothing store (J. Riggins) located in the town's one mall. It wasn't hard to be named No. 1 salesperson in a military town. Before I knew it, I was promoted to Floor Supervisor and that's when I moved out. I was 16 years old, and I found a tiny apartment that I could afford, and I was thrilled to be on my own. My dad gave me the old car that my sister used to drive, so I had everything I needed. I remember that I would unplug all the appliances when I left the apartment (except for the refrigerator, of course) because my dad used to complain about our *"sky high"* electric bills. I didn't care that it wasn't fancy. It was mine and I had a little peace of mind, for once.

I even got a second job at a used clothing store sorting clothes, except that I could not handle working with this one guy with special needs. He would talk to me all of the time, but he spit, drooled and had B.O. He reminded me of my mother after her shock treatments, except for the B.O. part, and it was too much for me to handle on a regular basis, so I quit.

That year, Mimi introduced me to one of her friends who played football for the local college. His name was [Bobby], and I guess you could say that he was my first true love, but he was from Texas, so when he moved away, things fizzled between us. I didn't even go to my high school prom because I wasted my time pining away over him. At that point, I decided that I did not want a career in retail, so I managed to save enough money to take some courses at the local college, but I hated Lawton so much that I could not take being there any longer. I then started to think about other places that I could go to college; other places that I could live and make a home for myself.

15 1/2-Year-Old Me

Clearwater, Florida

Chapter Six: The Great Escape – My LA Days

It wasn't all doom and gloom for me. When I graduated from high school in 1987, I decided to move to Los Angeles, California. One of the siblings of our former next-door neighbor in Lawton View had moved to LA years prior. I contacted her and asked if I could stay with her and her husband for a short period of time. They talked about it, and she called me back. Thankfully, they were kind and generous enough to let me live with them, until I got on my feet. I was ecstatic.

My mom was so upset that I was leaving [*"her"*], that she could not bear the thought of saying goodbye to me, so she refused to go to the airport when I left. Nikki, of course, had no problem saying good riddance to me, so she volunteered to take me to the airport. I remember her last words to me before I walked out of her sight, she said, *"see you in two weeks. You'll never make it!"* I flipped her the bird, while committing to myself that I would *"NEVER"* move back to Lawton under any circumstance.

I was so excited about the possibilities that awaited me in LA. I didn't aspire to be in the entertainment industry. I just wanted a chance to make a life for myself and leave the old one behind. I was too anxious to sleep, as I had a million thoughts racing through my head, mostly a bunch of *"what if's?"*, but there was a fire lit inside me, and I was not about to let anyone put it out! I was feeling hopeful for the first time in my life.

When the airplane banked over the Pacific Ocean towards LAX airport, I cannot describe the feeling of seeing all that water. I thought to myself that there were so many places in the world other than Lawton, OK, and I wanted to make this new place my home and visit those other places too!

The couple, [Richard] and [Lizette] were wonderful to me. Their home was beautifully situated in an affluent LA suburb. There was no yelling or fighting. They were kind to me. They were kind to each other, and they welcomed me like family, but I knew that six months would fly by, so when I got a job, I tried to save every dime that I made. Eventually, I was able to buy a small economical car. I tried the city bus but that was a nightmare. I learned a lot of Spanish words while riding the LA city bus, but mostly the vulgar ones. I was reading the Help Wanted Ads in the newspaper every day, while trying to be as quiet as possible so as not to not disrupt Richard and Lizette's everyday lives too much. I did many of the chores and cooked sometimes. I tried very hard to show my appreciation and gratitude, but I had a goal to move out ASAP. I was used to being alone, and I needed that private self-reflective time to stay balanced.

Then, one day, I answered an ad for a reservationist at a major airline and got the job! I worked in a very small cubicle in a building near LAX. I went through training and excelled in my position. I felt free to be away from Lawton and away from the toxicity of my family, my community, and . . . away from my mom, although she called me constantly while I lived there, and my answering machine was usually so full that no one else could leave me messages. Finally, I told her that I would call her on Sundays. It didn't stop the messages but at least I was trying to let her know that I was okay and that she didn't have to worry about me. She was indeed a worrywart and unfortunately, I inherited some of that. I had strong negative feelings towards her, but I still had respect for her role as my mother.

It was at this airline that I saw an advertisement on the employee bulletin board for a furnished apartment that was available and affordable. I did not know anything about the neighborhoods in LA and was not sure who to ask, so I just took a chance and prepared to move into this unknown area.

It was four months after I arrived in California, and I was very happy to be on my own with my private space. I was on my way to beginning my new life, but not without some challenges, of course.

I had an evening shift at the airline, so it was usually dark when I got home. One evening, I came home and found what appeared to be a couple of bums sitting on my back porch. I don't know if it was from a life of perpetual suicidal ideations or the fact that I grew up in a rough area or both, but strangely, I was not afraid. I said hello and went into my apartment, stepping around them both and I tell you, those same *"bums"* ended up watching my apartment for me when I was not at home, and watching my car at night. Sometimes, I would give them a dollar or two when I had it. I never had any issues with them or my apartment. They had made some bad choices in their lives, but it did not mean that they were bad people.

Another evening, I was walking up to my door after my shift ended and I heard a voice say, *"Whatchu wearing all that dead for*?!" I didn't even understand what that meant. I turned around and saw a group of young men all wearing blue bandanas. I explained that I was not from there and had just moved. As it turned out, I had moved into the Rolling Sixties Crip territory and wearing *"dead"* meant wearing the color RED. *"Oh crap. What the heck*?!" I apologized and said that I would not wear red again in the neighborhood and that was good enough for them. I showed no fear, and they never messed with me after that encounter.

Knowing that I could not just abruptly move somewhere else, I needed to make sure these guys knew that I was not stuck up, nor afraid of them and so I would say hello to them when I saw them. One day, they shared with me that they were glad that I was not afraid when I first met them.

They said when people came to their neighborhood and acted afraid, clutching their purses, etc., they *gave* them something to be afraid of by purposely messing with them, because it was insulting and disrespectful to them for people to just automatically assume the worst. I was not afraid of them, but I did start sleeping with a big knife under my pillow (just in case).

Since I was working for an airline, I had flying benefits, but I did not know who to visit or where to go, so I decided to take my first free trip back to Lawton. I was upgraded to first class and that was nice. I drank champagne, and I thought that it was so cool.

My mom and dad picked me up from the airport and my thoughts immediately raced back to my upbringing there. As soon as I saw them, I wanted to get back on the plane and leave.

When we got to the house, I was able to spend some time with my niece, Nikki's daughter, who she had when she was about 15 years old, so I was old enough to help raise her. At first, Nikki was observant and took her usual cheap shots at me to which I ignored, but then she launched into other attacks, saying that I was now "*talking white*" and that I thought I "*was better*" than them, none of which were true. My niece even started saying that her auntie was "*talking white*" and "*acting white.*" Yes, ignorant, I know, but I guess you can't blame them because they were taught to think that way. I was too, until I knew better, but you don't know what you don't know.

My mom was happy to see me and wanted me to spend all my time with her and that was suffocating enough. I had the same complete feeling that I had long ago when I felt trapped by fear and loneliness. The house had a familiar smell that was making me nauseous as it brought back so many painful memories. I suddenly remembered the times when my dad tied my mom up and it was during the winter months.

She was wearing shorts and a white tee shirt, and she had either a cold or the flu. She had gotten very violent and was spitting on the carpets. It was the smell of her phlegm that I was remembering, and I could not handle it. I cut my trip short and left after two days. Being back in Lawton had made me physically ill and I had a headache the whole time I was there. I could not wait to leave!

Back in Los Angeles, I exhaled with relief and enthusiasm. *Why did I even waste my time going back there?*

I worked at the airline for about a year and then I started dating. I was on a date one summer weekend when my date and I were stopped by the LAPD. The cops exited their car with guns drawn. They yanked my date out of the car and threw him to the ground. They made us get on our knees on the hot curb with our hands behind our backs and they proceeded to ask him if he had any drugs or weapons in the car. They looked at me and asked if I was Mexican. We were calm and I believe he got a ticket for something bogus, but that increased my fear of the police, because no matter how cooperative we were, they were extremely mean and rude to us for no reason. We could literally feel their hatred towards us. I remember thinking that if the police hate us this time, then who will protect us? I knew that my only protector would be God.

I eventually found a better job as a receptionist in a major law firm in Beverly Hills, California on Wilshire Boulevard. That was a blessing. I got a huge pay increase, which meant that I could do more things, including shopping, and I certainly had more options with men, because I could frequent more upscale establishments.

I met a very good friend at that law firm (my [celebrity-friend]). She was a legal secretary there at the time and she was always a hustler. If there ever was someone who dedicated 1000% to their goals, it was *her*. We have a true and sincere friendship.

Today, she has a successful talk show. She may be someone who you might see on your TV every day. One year, that law firm had a talent show and she performed as Tina Turner and won the first-place prize. I sang "*Hero*" by Mariah Carey and won the second-place prize, which I believe was $100. This celebrity-friend prayed with me and for me, so many times. I am thankful that she is still a part of my life.

I remember when we used to go to comedy clubs in LA and I would watch her perform as she drank her Shirley Temple, and I drank something stronger. It was fun to sit in the audience and watch her make people laugh. She was able to relate to people from all walks of life and bridge that gap through comedy, authentically.

It was around that time that I moved into a better neighborhood and that's when I met a couple of other friends. They were two sisters named [Kat] [deceased] and [Kim], and they became my best friends. I spent every Thanksgiving with them, their mother, brother, and grandparents as they welcomed me into their home. Those were some of the best memories in LA, just hanging out with them and experiencing normal family interactions.

I met a few A-list celebrities back then, and some of them before they got big, but I treated them like I would anyone else. For some reason, even coming from little Lawton, Oklahoma, I was comfortable in that environment, and not at all starstruck, well most of the time I wasn't.

Kat and Kim were also well connected in LA. Their mother was a successful businesswoman, who was able to give her children all of the finer things in life. I think they drove Porsches in high school, and it was through them that I met more celebrities, including going to a certain comedian/actor's pool party, where we saw and met other celebrities.

We even chilled in another well-known actor's trailer while he was filming a movie. He was very funny, but when he pulled out his humongous penis, I had to go.

I heard that later that evening, a few girls went back to his place, and it got interesting. When I told another friend of mine in the industry what had happened, she said, "*Girl, [his name] shows his dick to everybody.*" Just wow.

I know that some people are fascinated by the LA crowd. I found it entertaining but my traditional values never left me. So many people there are fake but there are a few real ones too. It was also very cliquish, and I was careful about choosing friends wisely. I never went out alone and if my friends and I were at a party, when the party seemed to end, but not really, just a few people hanging back, for the "*after party*" and when the drugs started to kick in, you could feel and sometimes smell it in the air, we would politely excuse ourselves and leave immediately!

I had a conversation with a certain celebrity on one occasion, and I asked her about how Hollywood might change a person. She gave me an example of how she was on the set of filming a TV show, and they were taking a break. She only slightly mentioned to herself out loud that she wished she had a mint and before she knew it, there was someone there with a fresh mint in hand just for her. She said some people tend to change around you, so sometimes you naturally change as a result. Interesting perception.

One of my fondest memories of living in LA was when I met the one and only, Richard Pryor. We had front row seats at the comedy show that night and when he arrived, he was with someone who I believe was his wife and she was helping him on stage. He sat in a chair and had a cane, which she sat against his chair. He was still funny, of course, but he just moved a little slower.

At one point earlier in the show, his cane fell to the floor, but no one moved to pick it up for him.

It was just silent and I looked to his [wife], then to security, but it was like everyone paused, so there I went, slowly bending down, picking up his cane ever so gingerly, and placed it back against the chair, before trying to get back to my seat unnoticed, when he looked down at me and said, *"Who the fuxx is she?"* in a way that only he could deliver. It was hilarious!

One year, I went to the Soul Train Music Awards. I was dressed up in my little black dress and went to an event that up until that point, I had only seen on TV. It was all very exciting. The Awards started and the host began to speak. Later in the show, guess who came walking through the door in his military gear with this entourage?! Tupac! The audience went CRAZY! The whole room shook with cheers and applause. He had an incredible presence.

I also remember going to the tapings of *Comic View* and people would call me and say that they saw me in the first row. I was having a well-deserved time of my life.

LA was a cool place to live during my twenties. California had a carefree mentality, and I fell in love with the beaches and sunshine. The sisters and I always had so much fun together and I was rarely depressed back then, but also, I rarely smiled. The pain and mistrust were always there, but I learned to mask it in front of people for fear of rejection or being called weird. In all of the pictures that we took together (there were about 5 of us in a group), I was always the one who really didn't smile, more like a fake smile and the only one not showing any teeth. I was able to conceal my occasional depression and anxiety, but sometimes, I still felt socially awkward, and I know they knew it, which made me feel even more self-conscious.

One night, Kat and I were at a club in LA called *"Safe Sex,"* and she introduced me to [Casanova]. He was tall, caramel brown, attractive, an entrepreneur, went to UCLA, drove a Porsche and was very charming. We hit it off from the beginning and that is who I dated for much of the time that I lived in LA. He treated me like a lady, gave me nice things and we went to nice restaurants and other very nice venues. We had some fun times, but as with most of my relationships, he was caught seeing other women, and subsequently, I walked away from him.

I remember going at another night club called *"The World"* and I met the lead singer of a popular 80's American R&B group. We went on a date to the beach and it was chill, but of course, he wanted to do more than just gaze at the ocean, so that was our one and only date.

LA was becoming more crowded and crazier, especially after the 1992 riots. Those were unnerving times. I lived on the top floor in a 5-story building that was gated. On the night of the riots, if you weren't in front of your TV, you were out on your patio or balcony listening to the chaos. Some dummy kept opening the gate while the rest of us were yelling at him to close it. I lived by myself, so I had to be ready for anything, and I was.

One day, I was at a red light when a guy came right up to my driver's side, opened my door and tried to pull me out. I floored my car and fortunately, did not wreck. Since that incident, I always lock my car doors!

Another time, I woke up to a police business card on my front door. At that time, I lived on the third floor in a nice apartment complex in a nice area just down the street from Venice beach.

The complex across from me was even nicer and they had a security guard, unlike ours.

Apparently, the night before, their guard had witnessed a man climb from balcony to balcony (*"like Spiderman"*) to my balcony, where he gained entry inside of my apartment. He was there for a while before the guard saw him existing with a pillowcase full of my property. He then dropped my bike that I had on my balcony, to the lower floor, crawled back down the balconies and rode off into the night with my things. It was a miracle that I didn't wake up because I am a light sleeper. Who knows what would have happened if I did. I don't think they ever caught the guy, but more importantly, I was okay, and the items that he took were easily replaced. However, I did not feel safe there anymore, so I moved again.

It was at that point that I decided to go back to school. I went to junior college in West LA, and it was always my intention to transfer my credits to a four-year university. It was good to be in school and learn new things. It was also a nice distraction from my negative thoughts and painful memories, because there was always something happening. I experienced my first earthquake (Northridge) while sitting in the library at school and studying for a test. I watched in amazement as a single chair rolled from one side of the room to the other and I could feel the earth move beneath me. That was crazy.

After some time, I was promoted from receptionist to legal secretary. I was working full-time and going to school part-time, so I was too busy to think about relationships, until one day, a man moved into my duplex. In fact, he moved directly across from me. His door was literally just a few feet in front of mine. Let's call him [Clarence]. He was also tall and handsome, but this time, I decided to take it slowly, especially since he was just getting out of a bad marriage (with two kids). He played professional football when he was younger, and he had a nice build. As a result, he knew many other retired professional football players, including one whom he shared a dorm with while they were in college.

We became good friends, and then eventually it evolved into a romantic relationship, but I was not truly happy or satisfied with him because I was not prepared to be a stepmother to two small children, especially with them calling me *"Santa's Helper"* due to my short stature and of course hearing the dreaded *"You can't tell us what to do, you're not our mother!"* so I started to pull back, but not before I accidentally discovered a secret.

Clarence was answering his door one evening when I was walking up to mine. There were two tall black guys that proceeded to walk into Clarence's apartment as he opened his door, and they were carrying a large brown shopping bag with the words *"Oak Tree"* on the outside (a men's clothing store that went bankrupt). They were behaving suspiciously, which caught my attention, so I started to walk towards Clarence's front door and that's when I saw what was in the bag. It appeared to be dark men's clothing with what appeared to be dark, reddish-brown stains on it that were dry, and something crusty, that looked like small pieces of human skin. Clarence quickly rushed to the door to push me back, but he later confirmed what I already knew; that these were the clothes of a very famous person, who was later acquitted of murder. Yes, it's who you think it is.

Eventually, I graduated with my degree in paralegal studies and later changed law firms for more pay. It was there that I met another lifelong friend. Her name was [Mary], and she was a legal secretary too. She was 12 years older than I was and I enjoyed talking to her because of her kindness and wisdom. She was a strong Christian woman who loved the Lord. She prayed for me and with me all of the time, and I allowed her to see parts of the real me, although I didn't tell her about my childhood horrors. She just knew that I was masking a lot of anger and pain.

I decided to leave that law firm for a smaller one, where I would be the office manager, as well as the legal assistant. It was a nice bump in pay, with more duties, which was fine with me because I was gaining more skills. Everything was great, until the owner started to sexually harass me. At first, he was subtle, but then he would casually touch my shoulder or back. We went to an accident site together one time, at a mall, and I casually commented about a certain pair of shoes. The next day, that beautiful pair of Cole Haan shoes were sitting in my office. This guy was married with kids, and I had no intention of having an affair with him. So, I quit, without the shoes.

At that point, I had been living in LA for about 8 years, and I was seriously considering moving again. Traffic was becoming almost unbearable, and the homeless population was increasing. It was then that I started to wonder if this was the place that I would call home. The thing that I loved best about LA was the beach. My friends and I would go there most weekends and there was a lot to see and do all the time! There were many vendors, many restaurants, many entertaining acts and a huge basketball court. Also, at the beach, they handed out free tickets to some of the live TV shows that were filmed at the local studios there, so I was able to see how they make sitcoms. That was really entertaining.

The ocean was the only place that gave me true peace, and I lived right down the street from it! It was so wonderful. Then, one day, I received a call from Lawton that my dad had had a stroke and was paralyzed on his right side. I wanted to stay in LA for a bit longer, but it was getting ridiculously expensive too, and my mom called me constantly saying that she needed my help, so I made the decision to relocate to Dallas, Texas. Dallas was a three-hour drive to Lawton. I figured that it was close enough to family but not too close. I was wrong, though.

The Comedy Store

Soul Train Music Awards   **Law Firm**

1996 – Goodbye to California

Chapter Seven: Relocation to Texas

I sold just about everything I owned in LA, and moved to Dallas, Texas. I lived with my friend Mimi, who had moved to Dallas after she graduated from college in Lawton.

I drove to Lawton and wanted to be there to help my dad. My parents were both getting older and needed some assistance, but I also had to focus on getting on my feet, so I would only go every other weekend.

I quickly found a job at a major law firm and got my own place. Mimi and I hung out a lot and I started to meet other friends too. It was not long before I was checking out the dating scene, and I met a professional football player at the Cowboy Cafe. He was from New York, and he was tall, dark, handsome, and charming. We dated for a few months, and it was fun. We went to a lot of places and people recognized him. It was interesting to me that this guy had a lot of money, but he was comped at so many of the places that we went to.

Then one morning, after spending the night at this place, I did a little snooping when he left for a meeting. Something that I had not done before, but I was curious, so I looked in a kitchen drawer and I found a list of girls' names, as if he was listening to voicemails and writing down who called -- Lisa, Ashley, Tiffany, Brandy, Jade, Destiny, and Ina. I guess I was a part of his Top Ten Roster. I was shocked. I thought I was special! He treated me like I was special, and I still believed that he genuinely cared for me, but I was really just another trophy to him, and my ego could not handle it, so I walked away. I guess I was being naïve to think that a young, handsome guy playing for the Dallas Cowboys would not be a player. Oh well. Another one bites the dust!

I was making decent money. I went shopping and tried to get on with my life. I had considered going back to school, but I was already working in the law field and already had the education to be a paralegal, so I guess I got complacent. I also wanted to avoid taking out massive student loans. In hindsight, I should have been focused on myself and gone back to college, but I was still struggling with my confidence and comfort level around people. I was not driven to succeed and had no real goals to become a modern-day woman with a specific lucrative career in mind or a deliberate plan on how to get there. I think I spent most of my mental energy just trying to stay strong and forget about the past. My aunt once told me that the man makes the living, and the woman makes the living worthwhile. I guess I also bought into the fairy tale – silly me.

It also would have been difficult for me to return to college when my mom was constantly calling me all of the time begging me to "*Come home!*" I hated listening to her voicemail messages. I was feeling hatred towards her, and I often wondered if she knew what she was doing when she was molesting me. We had never talked about it, and I was still angry. It felt like she had crippled me because I could not get past so many vivid memories, and it affected every aspect of my life. I could not get past the shame, guilt, and the overall neglect. I was not playing the victim. I just wanted to feel normal.

To escape my nightmares, I shopped. If I had plans to go out, I bought a new outfit each time. I tried to walk with pride, while masking every dark thought with a forced smile.

And, then I met [Ben]. It was at a pool party. I had on a white bikini, mixed with a few too many glasses of champagne. Not to sound like a broken record, but this guy was all those things and more – tall, dark, exceptionally attractive, charming, nice, a professional – he was the whole package but not exactly the modest type. As we began to get to know each other better, we ran into a serious roadblock.

I learned that he was the younger brother of Bobby. The guy that I had dated in my senior year in high school, and he was in college in Lawton. Oh, no!

We talked about it and we both knew that it would be wrong to continue to see each other, so we made a conscious effort to back off. Until one day, I got a call from him. He had a situation that forced him to find another place to live, and I offered him my couch.

As time went by, we became the best of friends. We went out together a lot. We went to restaurants, to clubs, to shows, but only as friends. I watched him pursue other women and he watched other men pursue me. I enjoyed his company, and he was very witty. He would not allow me to sulk and even during my low days of depression; he was always able to cheer me up by saying something funny. It was hard not to want more, but I could see that he was a real ladies' man. All the women wanted to be with him, and all the men wanted to be just like him.

We never really talked about bringing other men and women to the apartment. It was after all, *my* apartment but the truth was, I didn't want to bring any men home.

I guess you know that the inevitable finally happened. The attraction was undeniable. He said, "*Just say no and I'll stop.*" I didn't want him to stop. His brother eventually found out, but he didn't care. He was too busy juggling his own harem, so we continued to be intimate on occasion, but were still "*just friends.*"

Our friendship grew fast, and we were extremely close although we knew that we could never really have a relationship. He once said that if we had met first, that we would have probably been married by this time (was it just "*game*"? Probably).

Unlike his brother, Ben never made me feel bad about myself. Bobby would say that I had a funny shape. He was talking about my hip dints, and he "*jokingly*" would talk about other women right in my face, like about who they were ("*leasing agent*") and what they drove ("*candied apple red Porsche*"), which I found very disrespectful because he was clearly comparing me to them. At one point, we were discussing getting an apartment together and he actually said to me '*not to expect him to come home every night*'. *Really*? Ben may have been a dog too, but he was a good dog, very kind, gentle, generous, compassionate and considerate. It was inconceivable that I could keep my emotions intact and so one day, I came home and found what appeared to be the corner of a condom wrapper packet on my living room floor. He denied that it was his condom, but I knew better. A few days later, one of his "*thots*" told me that it was her who was at my apartment having sex with him on my living room floor. I asked him to leave, and we promptly ended our "*entanglement.*"

He never promised me anything and yet, I felt like my heart was broken, then I fell into another long depression. It was so hard to get out of bed each morning, but keeping a job and a roof over my head was more important. When you learn to rely on yourself, it's amazing how you can push past your depression, but it's not easy and it doesn't happen overnight. I don't know what came over me, but my sadness turned to anger, and I wanted revenge. So, I started hanging out with Ben's best friend just to try to hurt him. This guy was not my usual type at all, but I did it anyway just to hurt Ben. Unbeknownst to me at that time, he was a drug dealer and his name was [Cash]. He was big time.

Cash and I spent a lot of time together and I was shielded from his occupation for the most part. I started smoking weed with him and that became my self-medication, but my curiosity eventually got the best of me, and I asked him if I could try "*the white stuff.*" The first time I tried it, I remember staring at myself in the mirror and I said, "*Wow, I'm pretty*" and he replied, "*Now you can see what I see.*"

I was still functioning. I still had my job at the law firm, and I was still paying bills, with a little help from Cash of course. I was going to Lawton less and less. I knew better than to be with a drug dealer and to do drugs, but I kept doing it anyway. I loved the way it helped me to escape my reality. I had energy and felt alive. I didn't think about anything negative while I was high, and that worked for me, for a while.

We took a trip to Mexico one weekend and things changed after that. I did not ask any questions about why we were going there, and he did not volunteer any information. He always said that *the less I knew the better*. That was fine by me because I didn't want to know.

We made it to the hotel safely and I laid out by the pool, while he took care of his "*business*." The first night went smoothly but during the second night, there was loud banging at the door. The person identified themselves as the police and Cash quickly started to flush his product down the toilet. He eventually answered the door, but it was not the police. It was a security guard coming to let him know that someone had complained about the smell of marijuana.

The incident was so shocking to me, but it was the reality check that I needed. I never hung out with that type of crowd before. I never had friends that associated with drug dealers or did cocaine. *What was I thinking*? If I was going to try this kind of stuff and hang out with people who did that, I could have done it in Lawton or LA. So, when we got back to Dallas, I had to walk away from him and walk away from the thing that made me look at myself and believe that I was beautiful and worth something more, the thing that made me feel like I could accomplish anything, but more than anything else, it took away my fear.

As it turned out, walking away from Cash proved to be a very wise decision. He was later shot in the face after leaving a nightclub.

Chapter Eight: Attempt No. 3

I quit cocaine cold turkey, and I immediately began to feel the withdrawals. I was starting to feel irritable and agitated all the time, just a constant uneasiness. At night, I would punch my bedroom wall and wake up with bloody knuckles. I had the sweats and muscle aches, and my depression worsened. I started calling in sick at my job a lot and when I did go to work, I knew that I was not on my A-game. I thought that everyone could tell something was different and my paranoia consumed me. I avoided everything and everyone, including my mom and dad. I felt extremely sad and had no energy.

The holidays were approaching, and I was feeling worse about myself and about my life. I saw a bleak future ahead of me, and I did not want to live to see another holiday or spend another day or week with that big empty hole in my heart. I just wanted someone to tell me that everything would be okay, and I wanted to believe it. I had family nearby on my mom's side, but they reminded me of her so much that I wanted to avoid them too. Also, I did not want them to know that I was recovering from cocaine withdrawal, and I knew that they would be asking a lot of questions, so I stayed in my shell and put my plan into motion. I just couldn't take it anymore. I didn't want to take it anymore. And who the heck would miss me anyway?

There's a calm that comes over you when you've finally made up your mind to end your life. I put in my two-week notice at my job. I put in my 30-day notice at my apartment, and I wrote a letter to the bank letting them know where to pick up my car. I went to the hardware store and bought a drill, some drill bits and rope. I went to the grocery store and bought a bottle of sleeping pills and a bottle of wine.

I was 28 years old, and I had reached my limit. I made a mess of my life, and I didn't know how to clean it up.

It was the second week of November in 1997, and it was late at night, I think around 11:00 p.m. The more I drank, the more I cried and the more I had liquid courage. I took the entire bottle of sleeping pills and washed them down with the bottle of wine. I was sure this would be a good Plan B.

There were tall ceiling beams in my apartment, and I drilled a hole through one of them. Some kind of way, I threaded the rope through the beam and tied it securely, then I made a loop and tied a knot. I put a chair just underneath where the rope was hanging, and I stood on top of the chair. I was curious to know what it would feel like when it happened and so I gently lowered my neck onto the noose and firmly pressed down for just a bit with my feet still planted firmly on the chair. Things quickly started to get dark and so I figured that it wouldn't be so bad to just blank out before my neck is broken. I had fainted before. It's like someone turning the lights off and you're out.

I prayed to God for forgiveness and then I kicked the chair away from me.

The next thing I remember was around 2:00 or 3:00 a.m. and I was lying on the floor. My neck was bleeding from the rope burn. I felt sick to my stomach and started throwing up. I was having a hard time seeing clearly. I was immediately frustrated, and I started crying and yelling repeatedly, "*Why God, why are you keeping me here?*" and for the first time, I heard God speak to me. It's hard to describe, and I know it may sound bizarre to some who have never experienced it, but I tell you it's true. I did not hear him audibly, but I could clearly *feel* Him near me, deep within my soul. The Bible describes it as a "*small still voice*" referring to the Divine whisper heard by the prophet Elijah.

I could strongly feel him say, "*Stop this*! *You are not going anywhere until I say so*!" It is difficult to put into words but suffice to say that when God speaks, you know it's Him without a doubt. I was immediately humbled and fell to my knees begging Him for forgiveness. I had thrown in the towel and God threw it back! I still didn't understand why he was keeping me around, but I was starting to feel like there had to be a purpose for me to be here.

Once the adrenaline wore off, I started to really feel the pain from the burn on my neck, I was still dizzy and nauseous. The rope was still around my neck, and it was also still attached to the beam, almost like someone had cut it in the middle, but I lived alone, and no one had keys to my place. I sat there on the floor scratching my head and then I looked up to God and said, "*Thank you*."

Eventually, I was able to call my friend Mimi, and she came and took me to the hospital. She was mad at me too, but all I could do was sit there with my head in my hands in shame, still trying to see through my blurred vision.

At the hospital, they, of course, asked me a million questions and then they gave me a liquid form of charcoal. It was disgusting and they watched me while I drank every drop of it, which was used to make me throw up. They treated the burn on my neck and admitted me that night. Someone came to my room that night and wanted to talk about why I did it, but I wasn't ready. Then, when I was out of physical danger, someone different came to my room to tell me that I would be transferred to the local mental hospital. I asked what would happen if I refused to go and they said that I would be physically forced to go due to a court order that had already been obtained. All of my life, I had waited to become my mother and there I was, being forced to go to a mental hospital, just like her.

Chapter Nine: That Major Disappointment

The first thing they did was make me change into their hospital attire. I felt humiliated that they had two women in the room watching me the whole time and checking my hair, and other parts, then they escorted me to my room that I would be sharing with another female patient, and they told me that I would be on a 24-hour suicide watch that evening.

The facility was like a big circle of rooms with tables and chairs in the middle. We had one-on-one sessions in the middle of that room with a doctor who looked like a kid. I called him "*Doogie Howser*," and he would always ask the same questions, including, "*Are you thinking about hurting yourself?*" Of course, I thought about suicide every day, but I was telling him otherwise because they did not separate the troubled patients from the *really* troubled patients. If I wasn't crazy already, being in that place was going to drive me crazy.

There was a big black guy there who ran around naked, and he came up to everyone with his hand cupped, appearing to try to hand them something but nothing was in his hand. He would just say, "*Here ya go, Bo.*" That was a distraction.

There was a woman there who saw snakes and would often scream. During the first night, my roommate got up in the middle of the night and turned the light on, then she got back into her bed. She got up again and that time, she turned the light off. She did this another time or two, then she jumped out of bed and yelled, "*Who the fuxx keeps turning the light on*?!" I stayed ready for anything.

There was another day that this female patient kept trying to talk to me and befriend me. She said that she was a palm reader and wanted to read my palm, but I just wanted her to go away, then one day, I got so sick of her that I said, "*If I let you read my palm, will you leave me alone?*" She said, "*Yes*" and so I foolishly put out my hands. She looked down at them, looked up at me, looked down at them again and then walked off. Not long after that, one of the technicians came up to me and said that they were putting me on another 24-hour suicide watch. When I asked "*why?*" They told me that the other patient had read my palms and saw that I would try to commit suicide again. *Are you freaking kidding me?!* They're listening to the girl who also thinks she's a fairy?! I think the people that worked there might have been off their rockers too.

I had to get out of that place, so I decided to start going to the group sessions. We said The Serenity Prayer and we were encouraged to share our problems with each other, but I never felt comfortable doing that, so mostly, I just listened and kept to myself. There were so many unstable people in the facility, but I guess I was not making much progress myself, as I refused to talk about my issues. Every day that I didn't talk about my issues, they wrote it down in my file, and I was further away from getting out of there. Then one day, I finally decided to privately share a little with one of the mental health technicians. That decision caused me further pain down the road, but as we know, hindsight is 20/20. I believe it is fitting to refer to him as [Damien]. Damien came up to me and said, "*Just tell me it wasn't because of a guy*" and I answered "*Nope.*" He asked what had brought me to the decision to end my life and I told him that my mother was schizophrenic to which he replied, "*And, my dad is bi-polar, so what?*" And that started a conversation that I had hoped would be sufficient for the counselors. Damien introduced me to a new term "*The Power of the Pen*" and it was a reminder to me that the staff was writing down everything I said and did.

Damien had a later shift that ended around 11:00 p.m. and he spent a lot of his evening talking and listening to me. Physically, I was not attracted to him at all. He was on the shorter side, brown-skinned, with a peanut head. He was the type of guy that I would not give a second look outside of those hospital walls and I certainly did not read anything into our conversations. I did not tell him everything about me, but I told him enough that I began to feel vulnerable with him. They had been giving me different medications from the first day, and I was really hoping that they would give me energy and make me happy, but instead, they just flattened me out and made me feel loopy.

He came to my room almost every night to say goodbye to me at the end of his shift. I would be sound asleep sometimes, as would my roommate (after she cut off the light for the last time), then I would see a light come through the cracked door with him peering inside, seeing if I was awake. I'm pretty sure that he wasn't supposed to be doing that, but at that point, he was still being somewhat professional, and I was still trying to give him something substantial to write into my file, like I was cooperating and going along with the process.

Our conversations eventually became personal, and he told me that he was married, but separated and that his wife abandoned him and moved to another state. I was relieved to hear that he was married because that was definitely a *"NO-NO"* for me. I told him about the guy (Ben) who I was kind of dating but more like friends with benefits, who hurt me and that's when he gave me the old, *"if I was your man"* line. I was like, *"Uh no. Just stop!"* I had absolutely zero intention of hooking up with that guy.

I was there for a few weeks and towards the end of my stay, I had to decide how to restart my life again but this time, I felt like God was with me and wouldn't let me fail.

Although, I still didn't really have a place to go to and didn't want to burden Mimi any more than I already had. I also didn't really feel close enough to my mom's side of the family to call them and abruptly disrupt their lives, so against my better judgment, I agreed to stay at Damien's place until I could figure something out.

Damien was in the process of planning a move to Atlanta, and I was focused on figuring out a way to stay alive and have a life worth living, and then it happened. I made a mistake and slept with him. It was not love. It was not romance. It was just a girl and a boy alone, resulting in an unplanned pregnancy. I take full responsibility, medicated or not, I knew better.

In a matter of a couple of months, he had filed for divorce, was packing to go to Atlanta, and asked me to marry him. I felt like I was in the *Twilight Zone*, and I was so confused. What else was I going to do? I didn't have a job, a car, or any money. I didn't want to have an abortion. I figured that no guy would ever want me, knowing all of my flaws and terrible family secrets. The last time I checked, "*crazy*" was never an attractive quality and so I threw caution to the wind, and followed him to Georgia, stopping in Columbia, South Carolina long enough to get married at some chapel on the side of the road. I literally stuttered through my vows, and I don't stutter. I even asked the preacher to repeat himself at one point. Everything in me was screaming **DON'T DO IT**, but I didn't listen. I felt stuck and I started to justify the marriage. At least I wouldn't have to call him "*My baby's daddy*," and he did do some pretty cool magic tricks, but as we know, magic is based on illusion.

Initially, we moved in with his cousin, who lived in the suburbs of Atlanta. I got a job at a bank instead of a law firm because they were all located in downtown Atlanta, and we were having car problems at the time. I liked the suburbs, and I just wanted a simple life.

Damien got two jobs, one at a dry cleaner down the street and another at a warehouse. He had been in the Marine Corps, but he didn't seem to have any real marketable skills. He told me that he went to Southern University and so I assumed that with at least some college education, he would be able to have some better options, but that didn't turn out to be the case.

I was reading the Bible one evening and asked him to read the next chapter. It was only then that I realized that he barely knew how to read. I guess I should have started with Dr. Seuss' *Green Eggs and Ham*! When we were around other people, he would act differently, trying to impress them, even if that included lying and name dropping. It was a total turn off for me. It was becoming clearer and clearer that we really didn't know each other at all. We were polar opposites and had no business being together, but I was going to make the best of it, and I was excited to be a mother and was determined to be a great mom. We lived in Georgia for about one year and during that time, I paid for him to go to barber school so that he would at least have a trade. I considered a job in the law field but once I had my first son [Justin], I wanted to spend as much time with him as I could. This little baby saved my life, because I took one look at him, and I knew then that suicide was no longer an option for me.

Damien graduated from barber school and found a job as a barber at a black-owned salon. It didn't bother me that he was around women all day because I was in a loveless marriage and we both seemed content to stay that way.

I was so worried about leaving Justin at the daycare center, that I changed my hours at the bank to part-time and got a part-time job at his daycare center as a teacher's aide. Damien was becoming more and more distant at home, and my gut instinct told me that he was cheating with one of the owners, who was married to a professional football player that traveled all the time.

I didn't want to be the jealous wife and I'm not sure I cared that much, so I just gave all of me to Justin, and treated Damien like a roommate.

I did not like Georgia much. There was more racism there than in Oklahoma. It seemed that the white people there hated black people, and the black people hated them just as much, but also hated *other* black people. It seemed segregated by choice. We were in church one day and I almost got into a fight with a black guy, who was acting hysterical and yelling at me to go outside with my crying baby (Justin). I did take him outside but when he stopped crying, we came back inside and sat down in the back temporarily, when this guy started going off on me, telling me that the back seats were reserved for ushers only but there was no Usher sitting there at that moment. He got so loud with me that I just snapped (in church!) and asked a stranger to *"Hold my baby"* (ready to physically fight this man). I told him that he was acting ghetto and that he was messing with the wrong person. The Pastor stopped mid-sentence and wanted to know what was going on in the back of the church. Everyone turned around and then I saw Damien turn around and say, *"Uh oh, that's my wife."* The Pastor invited us to visit with him in his office and told a deacon to take over for him. It turned out, they had a lot of problems with that particular church member. He had tried to organize a strip show for Mother's Day and that did not go over well with the congregation. He was asked not to return, but someone later decided to give him another chance.

Another day, Justin's class went on a school field trip, and I volunteered to chaperone. I think it was to a farm or something but what I really remember about that trip were all the confederate flags that I saw on the way to the location, and I felt very unsafe.

On a separate occasion, I took Justin to the park to play, and a white lady called her son away from my son.

Justin wondered why he could not play with this kid, and it was obviously because Justin had brown skin.

I decided then that I did not want to raise him in the South, so I told Damien that I wanted to leave Georgia, and we discussed our options.

He mentioned some tourist town on the east coast where some guy had offered him a job managing a resort, and he also mentioned Miami. He was very excited about the possibility of moving to Miami. For me, the North was out of the question because I did not like the cold, and the same thing went for the east coast. I absolutely excluded any southern states, so that really just left the west coast and I was thinking of Arizona or Oregon.

I was working at a major bank as an Executive Assistant to one of the Vice Presidents in that region, and I met a wonderful woman there who worked out of their Phoenix, Arizona location. She was older and had raised her two sons alone too. We just hit it off. Then, the bank sent us to Columbus, Ohio for training and we met in person. Her name was Ijrih, and it was great to finally be able to hang out with her. She was full of wisdom, and I learned so much from her. We were very close, and she became more like an aunt than a co-worker/friend.

She had a lot of good things to say about Phoenix, and I thought it might be a good idea to get a fresh start there. I talked to Damien about it, but he was really pushing for Miami, Florida. One day, I told him that we needed to decide one way or another because I hated the South and so, there we sat and instead of preparing divorce papers, we were writing the city and state of our choice on a piece of paper and placed it in a hat. We each took the paper of the other and read it aloud – both pieces of paper read "*Arizona*."

In April of 2000, we packed up another moving truck and headed for Phoenix, Arizona.

65

I found an apartment there online while still in Georgia and I was set up for an interview that week from a legal placement service that I also found online.

Everything fell into place. We completed our move. I was offered and accepted the job at my first interview at a large, reputable law firm. Damien got a job at a local barber shop, and we enrolled Justin into a nice daycare center nearby.

After about a year, we bought a new house. It had just been built, and I was happy to finally have some space. Damien and I were going through the motions as usual. I remember going to church one day, the three of us, and I saw him flirting with some young girls right in front of me. When I looked up, he was smiling, and the girls were laughing. He started to lose all respect for me and became verbally abusive, calling me fat and telling me that if I left that no one else would want me. It was control, but I believed him. I still didn't like myself, and I allowed him to tear me down further.

In 2001, things really went sour when he got a new job. He was staying at work later and later and was missing in action a lot. Even on holidays, he just didn't seem to want to be there and was always tired. All the signs were there that he was cheating. The first sign was when I noticed that he was not wearing his wedding ring. When I asked him about it, he said, "*I don't like jewelry.*" So, I responded, "*You know, I don't really like jewelry either*" and I promptly took my wedding ring off that day, which I later pawned.

I moved my things into the spare bedroom and let him have the master bedroom all to himself. Even the occasional sexual contact had completely ceased. I don't think either of us had the desire for one another, and it was because of Justin that I stayed for as long as I did.

I knew that things would play out exactly the way they were supposed to, so I waited for the other shoe to drop and hoped that I would be ready when it did.

I stopped doing his laundry and stopped cooking for him. It was a sad existence, but Justin was my baby, and we started going to the matinee movie on Sundays and avoiding Damien like he was avoiding us. Everything I did, I did with Justin by my side, and I was content with that for a little while. The Bible allowed me to divorce Damien due to adultery but instead of looking for evidence, I knew that the truth would eventually be revealed.

At some point, my occasional depressive moods that usually came and went were now lingering again. I struggled for weeks, and I didn't want Justin to see me that way, so it was then that I voluntarily started taking anti-depressants. They helped somewhat, but I was tapping into sheer will to keep myself going for my son's sake.

Then one day, I didn't get my cycle, and I went to the doctor. To my surprise, the doctor walked in and told me that I was pregnant. I quickly said, "*How?*" "*By who?*" I was literally in shock! I was sure that they had made a mistake, so I took another test, and it was positive. WTH?! I went home and told Damien that I was pregnant, and he had the same response, "*By who?*" It is wild to know this, but apparently, neither one of us had remembered the one time that we were together and that one time was all it took - but how? Did he drug me, and I didn't remember? I was having another baby with him. I was *not* happy, and he acted like he could care less, saying that it wasn't his baby.

I turned half of the spare bedroom into a nursery as I prepared for the baby's arrival. Damien never went to any doctor's appointments with me and again, was never at home, but I kept pushing on.

If he didn't want to be involved, it was his loss and sooner or later, I would find the strength to leave him.

In December of 2002, I had my youngest son, [Andrew]. Damien managed to make it to the birth just in time. I had to have a second cesarean section due to the suicide attempt/car accident that I had when I was 14 years old. My pelvic bone grew back crooked and as a result, neither of my children was able to drop down low enough for regular delivery. I was awake during the entire delivery just like before.

When he came out of my belly, they took him away and I could immediately tell that something was different this time. I asked if he had all his fingers and toes and Damien answered, "*Yes.*" I kept asking what was wrong and they just kept saying that they couldn't open his left eye. I tried not to panic. In the ultrasounds, it just looked like his eyes were closed and now they're saying that they can't open one of them. I couldn't understand why. They said that they had to take him, and I didn't even really get a good look at him before everyone quickly left the room.

I was moved to another room and after some time, the doctor came in and told me that Andrew was born without a left eye. He had a rare disorder known as Microphthalmia with clinical Anophthalmia, which is Greek for "*No Eyes.*" The doctors called it a fluke, but I blamed myself for the anti-depressants that I started taking when we first arrived in Arizona (even though I later learned that there was no connection between the anti-depressants and Andrew's condition). They said that he would have to take several tests, including an MRI and CT-scan. They wanted to check for any cognitive effects. He was also born with a large bump on the left side of his forehead. At first, they thought that it was the eye that did not descend to the eye socket, but it turned out to be a lipoma or some other type of fatty tissue and he also had a cleft nose.

I cried all night. Was I being punished for something? I was honestly scared to death. Could I do this on my own? There was even one nurse there that gave me the option of leaving Andrew at the hospital to pursue adoption possibilities. I couldn't believe what I was hearing, and I felt devastated, but then a calm came over me. I felt love and peace, and I knew that God had chosen *me* to be Andrew's mom. Maybe everything that I went through up to that point in my life was to prepare me to be the mom that Andrew needed.

Damien left but he came back later. He didn't know what to say to me but naturally, he questioned the paternity, and he wasn't showering Andrew with much love and affection. He told me that he couldn't have a son that looked like that and so, I was on my own. After we were released from the hospital, I started doing research on his disorder and what I could do to help him. I found an Ocularist and Ocular Plastic Surgeon. It turned out that this particular plastic surgeon was familiar with Anophthalmia and had treated children born with it during his time in the Middle East. He was on a team of physicians that created a specific tissue expander that would enlarge the eye-socket area from the inside to stimulate the muscles and nerves to grow enough where he could eventually wear a prosthetic eye.

Andrew had his first surgery at 6 months old, and 7 surgeries later, they were able to stretch the tissue and open the eye wide enough for a prosthetic eye but since those were so expensive, we had to settle for a conformer. It was like a hard-shell contact lens, and it was blue. We called it his *"bionic eye."*

Four years passed and nothing had changed in my marriage. He was still doing his own thing, and I was still working and taking care of the boys and the home. Damien and I only communicated when it was absolutely necessary, like about a plumber, or something like that. I didn't miss him, and he clearly didn't miss me either.

It was in 2006 when I had a life-changing conversation with my mom. I told her that I was sick of living the way I was living, but she wanted me to try and work it out with Damien for the sake of the kids, and she talked about the headache of starting all over with someone new. Things were so bad for so long, how could they ever change when I didn't really want them to? She told me to try being sweet to Damien. Greeting him at the door after work, giving him a big hug and kiss and asking him about his day, things like that. I told her that I would give it a try. It worked almost immediately. He started coming home and paying more attention to me and the boys. I really wanted him to be a good father more than anything else. I didn't want my brown-skinned boys to grow up without a father, even if he wasn't around a lot.

Then, one day, after returning to work after a Fourth of July holiday weekend where the four of us, dressed in matching red, white and blue tee shirts, went to the park to enjoy the fireworks. I got to my desk and saw that I had a voicemail message. It was a woman's voice, a white woman's voice. I listened to the message a few times. I even transcribed the message just to make sure that I heard it correctly. It was something to the effect of, "*You don't know me, but I've been having an affair with [Damien] for the last four years. I'm sorry but we both were deceived.*"

Chapter Ten: The Three Musketeers

My head was spinning. First, there's the initial shock. It's one thing to suspect your husband of cheating but it's a complete other thing when it's staring at you right in the face.

I had just started a new job and now I was telling my bosses that I had to leave due to a family emergency. I didn't even call him. I just grabbed my purse and left.

When I got home, he was there. I simply told him that his little girlfriend had called me at my job and that I was throwing his ass out! I started pulling his clothes and things out of the closet and drawers and throwing them into the garage as he was putting them back and that went on for a while, back and forth from the bedroom to the garage with me telling him to "*Get the fuxx out!*" I was so angry, but not like broken-hearted, more like my ego was being fed through a shredder. *Why didn't he just leave me?*

I had waited for this day to come for years, and I was more than ready to move on with my life, whatever that entailed. I considered it karma, because Damien was married when we got together, so as far as I was concerned, I deserved it, but I begged for forgiveness and asked God to help my boys and I to start a new life, one filled with overflowing happiness.

When he eventually left that night, I had the locks changed. When he later came back home, he literally broke the door off the hinges, and while I was trying to forcibly get him out, he was holding me tight by my arms trying to make me listen to him. He was holding on with such a tight grip that he left bruises all over my arms.

She called me on Monday, and I filed for divorce on Friday of that same week. That's how sure I was that I wanted out of that marriage.

Over the next four months, he tried to beg me to stay, but so many things started to come to mind. Like the time I went to this fish and chips restaurant in downtown Phoenix. When the owner and I started to discuss a certain barber shop and I told him that my husband worked there, he turned white as a ghost and told me that he had met [Damien]'s wife and I wasn't her. That dummy was taking her around the city, introducing her as his wife, while I was at home taking care of our two children. I got played big time.

I had also wondered why our baby-sitter abruptly stopped coming around. She later told me that it was because she knew about the affair and couldn't face me. The people at his job even acted funny when I came around. I guess it's true that the cheated-on spouse is always the last one to know.

Here's *his* side of the story:

> It was uncommitted sex on the side, and apparently, she was willing to do *ANYTHING* sexually with him. He said that when I started to be nice to him again, he told her that he lied to her, and never really had any intention of leaving his family. When he told her that, she harassed him and threatened to tell me everything. Even if I didn't love him, he said he had enough love for both of us and that we owed it to the boys to stay together until Andrew was 18 years old.

Here's *her* side of the story:

> [Becky] was his boss at a mediocre barber/beauty shop
> franchise, and he came on to her, telling her that he had
> an open marriage. They started an affair that lasted
> four years (so, it started when I gave birth to Andrew).
> She said she purposely bought a house in the
> subdivision next to where we lived and that he lived a
> double life. She produced letters from neighbors,
> stating that they thought he lived there and had seen
> him on multiple occasions checking the mail, walking
> the dog, taking out the trash, etc. She produced letters
> from her mom and other family members and friends,
> stating that they had a long-term relationship and were
> engaged because he promised to leave his family one
> day. She even gave me a business card from a jewelry
> store where he bought her an engagement ring. She
> told me that when I traveled to Oklahoma the one time
> that I did with my boys so that they could meet their
> grandparents, they took that opportunity to fly to
> Montana to meet her family. I remembered that he was
> late picking us up from the airport and that he looked
> disheveled. She said that she started washing his
> clothes when I stopped and that she would find
> numbers in his pockets and would call these other
> women. One woman supposedly told her, "*[Damien]
> is MY man. You ain't his wife either*!" She was so
> humiliated that she stopped calling them. She also said
> that each year, they went to their company holiday
> party together, while telling me that it was for
> employees only. She said that he was even once
> accused of sexual harassment at a past job and that she
> helped him get out of it. She even told me about him

cheating with his old boss in Georgia. She went on to ask me about staying at a certain hotel for New Years Eve one year. He had gotten a second job at a hotel and was likely using the rooms to have sex with other women. On this New Years Eve, he kept leaving the room and coming back.

She was in an adjacent room apparently and he used that opportunity to spend NYE with both of us. She said that his (more like "*their*") nickname for me was "*Izza*," meaning "*Ina is a bitch*." Isn't that special? Oh, and she also told me that he threw his wedding ring out of the car window in an attempt to reassure her.

I mean, she knew more about the guy than I did.

It all made sense. He was a lying POS and a horrible human being, and I couldn't wait to get away from him. It was worse than I thought, but I knew that I would find out one day and that one day had *finally* arrived.

Well, when he understood that I was fed up and *DONE*, he got angry and called me crazy. He said, good luck finding someone who wants to deal with a "*one-eyed kid*," and he promised to make me suffer because of me leaving him. Fortunately for me, I insisted on having separate bank accounts. Each of our cars were in our own individual names so that would be easy to resolve, but since he refused to leave the home, I took the boys and got an apartment, and I let him buy me out of the house. I left everything except for our personal belongings. I literally could have cared less about furniture or anything of monetary value in that house because I knew that those things would be replaced, but not my time.

Later, I learned from a former neighbor that after we moved out, his mistress was seen staying overnight. They later married and had two children. I understand they are divorced now.

Moving on, Justin was eight years old, and Andrew was four years old. I took them to a local pizza place to break the news to them. We were going to be moving out of our three-bedroom/two-bathroom house into a small two-bedroom/one-bathroom apartment and that we would be moving without their dad.

Justin started to cry and said, *"I knew it, I knew it!"* Apparently, he had taken Justin and Andrew to her house to meet her, and Damien told Justin not to tell me. Justin told me that they were sitting at her kitchen table when she asked him *if he liked school?* and then she asked him, *"Who was his best friend?"* When he answered, *"My mom is my best friend,"* she supposedly ran out of the room crying.

I was furious that my son had to carry that secret for so long and I wanted to confront Damien, but it would not have mattered since he had proven himself to be a pathologically lying narcissist. The best thing we could do at that point was look ahead to our future and if Damien wanted to be a father to them, he was welcome to do that, but I was not going to spend my time trying to convince him to be one. We got the heck out of there fast and I didn't look back.

I really was quite terrified and didn't know how I was going to do it, but my boys needed me, and I needed them too, so we formed a union, calling ourselves the *"Three Musketeers"* and we were there for each other throughout this process of starting over and creating new memories, new traditions; just the three of us this time.

The four-plex that we moved into was an old building, which we later referred to as *"the Pit,"* was previously used by people that lived in Northern, Arizona, but escaped the cold for the sunny Phoenix weather. They are often referred to as *"snowbirds."*

For the first year, Damien did not give me one dime. He would say that he was waiting for the court to tell him how much to pay and I would say that his kids still needed to eat. I guess this was one way to *"punish"* me and teach me a lesson for leaving him, but Damien wasn't just punishing me. Both boys had a very hard time adjusting to the divorce and they were confused by why it had to happen and why he was choosing not to spend time with them.

He rarely saw Justin and Andrew and didn't even bother to call to see how they were doing. Then, I learned that his mistress was pregnant and so I guess he didn't have time for the children that he already produced. It was cool though, because we were the Three Musketeers and we were going to make it without him. I was determined to break some generational curses by loving and encouraging my children, so they became my sole focus. There was no dating. I was still very angry, and I wanted Damien and his mistress to experience a little pain too.

I decided to research adultery and what it all meant. Why do people do it? Don't they understand what they're risking and what it does to the children? I came across a very interesting book, entitled, *"Never Satisfied: How & Why Men Cheat"* by Michael Baisden. I learned so much about men from that book, but my newfound understanding did not diminish my anger. I didn't want him, but I was pissed that he made me look like a damn fool. I felt absolutely humiliated. While they were having all this kinky sex, why did they have to discuss me? He told her everything about me. I had no cards to play against her. I wanted blood.

I found an Arizona law against adultery. It is rarely prosecuted, but it is still against the law and on the books. Under Arizona law, adultery is defined as a married person engaging in sexual intercourse with someone who is not their spouse. The statute states that both parties involved in the act can be charged if one or both are married. It is classified as a class 3 misdemeanor. Imagine them getting served with legal documents that stated they were being charged with a crime! I wish I could have been a fly on the wall. Of course, I dropped the matter later after I found out that she was pregnant.

I could feel myself getting overwhelmed. This was not going to be an easy task, but other women raised their children on their own. I had a good job paying good money, so I thought to myself, if they could do it, so can I. I got myself together and forced myself to stand tall. What motivated me the most was to give my sons something that I didn't have. I wanted them to have a chance to have a happy life. I heard someone say once, that *"You never know how strong you are, until being strong is your only option."*

In many ways, I didn't have much of a childhood myself, so I just got silly with them. I was swinging on the swings with them, sliding on the slide at the park with them, playing hide and go seek right along with them, and playing video games. I mean, I genuinely enjoyed playing games with them, racing cars with Justin (*"vroom"*) and playing with wrestling action figures with Andrew (*"pow"*). We watched cartoons and stayed up late on the weekend watching movies.

I was no stranger to living a modest life and eliminating the non-essentials just to survive, but there were many good times too. My boys and I have so many fond memories and even though we never traveled very far, we still went on road trips to see so many different things.

On one family vacation, we drove to Las Vegas, Nevada. I had a strict budget. I carried a certain amount of cash with me and had a couple of credit cards. We went to a show, had room service every day, and had an absolute ball. As the trip was winding down, I realized that I had run out of cash and misplaced my credit cards. I tried not to panic but we certainly did not have one single person in the world that we could have called to help us. Things got real, real fast. I calmly explained to them that we needed some money, but I assured them that we were gonna be okay no matter what.

We went to the Strip and Andrew danced on the street corner for money. Justin helped too, but people wanted to see the little guy dancing. Andrew paid for dinner that night, took pictures with parrots and took care of everything we needed to get back to Phoenix. He made so much money that we had some left over! God continues to amaze me.

We were enjoying the simplicity of life because we were grateful for what we had, which was each other. It was rough at times, and I was exhausted a lot, but I was happy to wake up in the mornings. Doing so gave me the energy to keep moving and the motivation to help my sons to be emotionally healthy.

In 2007, we went to court to finalize the divorce. The judge was a Hispanic female, who was apparently captivated by Damien's perceived charm. She allowed him to introduce into evidence hand-written pay stubs that showed an extremely low salary, which was untrue, resulting in the judge awarding the boys $150 a month each for child support! Talk about a travesty of justice! She let him go on and on but kept cutting me off and calling me bitter. I wasn't bitter, I was mad as hell!

The child support was calculated by a formula. The more parenting time he was credited, the less that he would have to pay, but it turned out that he had no real interest in spending time with the boys, so he rarely exercised his parenting time. They saw him on rare occasions and only when Damien decided that he had time for them, including the one time that he took Andrew to the doctor to have a DNA test, because he insisted that Andrew was not his biological son. Of course, the paternity test determined that…he *WAS* the father (in my best talk show host voice).

It was not easy for us, especially when our small two-bedroom apartment flooded with backed up sewage water about an inch and a half, normally once a year due to roots from surrounding trees clogging up the plumbing. The owner was a slumlord who lived in LA and avoided putting any additional money into improving the building. There was a small laundry room with two washers and two dryers that sometimes worked and sometimes didn't, so we would routinely spend most of our Saturdays at the laundromat across the street.

The unit was awful for sure, but a wonderful thing happened there one night. During Andrew's many surgeries to reconstruct the left orbital area, a device was implanted to try to keep his left eye open. We wanted to purchase a prosthetic eye for him, but the cost was out of my price range and asking Damien would have been a colossal waste of time and so, I prayed, and I prayed for a miracle.

It was late evening on December 24, 2008, Christmas Eve. The boys and I were watching Christmas movies when we heard jingle bells. It sounded like they were on the roof. We were looking at each other in amazement, like *"What the heck is that?"* Someone knocked on the door and when I answered it, it was an older man and woman, dressed as Santa Claus and Mrs. Claus. They gave Andrew a check for the exact amount that we needed to get him a prosthetic eye. I kept looking up at their faces trying to figure out who they were but nothing about them seemed familiar. Someone made a little boy's Christmas wish come true and to this day, we have no idea who that mystery couple was, but if you are out there, *THANK YOU*. God is so good and that is why in my darkest of days, I continue to trust the Lord no matter what.

Some days were wonderful like that Christmas Eve night, but there were days that I felt defeated like I wasn't doing enough. I continued to be hard on myself because I wanted to give the boys the material things that they wanted and of course, everything that they needed but it was very hard sometimes. I remember one morning, I was crying in my bedroom, and Andrew came into the room. He put his little two hands on my face and said, "*Mommy, be strong.*" That was enough to snap me out of it. Later, they both told me that they could hear me crying in the shower some nights.

I took Justin to counseling first since he was the oldest, but he wanted no part of it. I would take him anyway and he would just put his hoodie over his head, slump into his seat and refuse to participate in the conversation. *He asked that counselor how could he help him when he had a weight problem*? We didn't go back there again. Justin was just so angry.

They were both in private Christian school at the time and Justin had a new teacher in his classroom. He started to lash out at her, saying, "*my parents didn't get divorced until you got here!*"

I took Andrew to counseling too. After seeing this psychologist for about a year, he said that he didn't think that he could help Andrew. Why? Because he had fallen in love (with me). Yikes!

I also researched a few mentoring programs but there was always a waiting list at least a year long.

During this time, I chose to seek out therapy for myself, but after going about three or four times, I didn't feel like it was helping me at all. In fact, it caused me more stress because I was taking time out of my day and missing work. I realized after that brief experience that finding the right counselor and establishing a rapport friendly enough to start sharing all my dirty laundry could take years. Instead, I found a non-denominational church home.

We went every Sunday and Justin and Andrew were baptized there but as they got older, things got harder.

In 2009, we were awakened around 4:00 a.m. by shouting and broken glass (*"Police, open up*!!). It was the police and immigration enforcement officers who were raiding the unit next to us, and several illegal immigrants were jumping out of the windows to get away. They filled that paddy wagon with more than 20 people. There were cartons of soda and many car seats that had been removed from cars and placed in the unit. I knew that something was up because I would hear noises in the middle of the night, water running and just a lot of moving around. I thought it was all strange, but I tried to mind my own business. After that incident, I knew that we had to move.

I was so desperate to move that I went to two payday loan companies to get $1,000 to finance the move. I didn't want to just move to another low-income apartment, so I waited until Damien sold the house to buy me out and I was able to use that money to put down on a home for me and my boys. It was a beautiful house, with a pool, gazebo, jacuzzi, fireplace and a large great room. I loved that house and we have so many fond memories there. We had a party for just about every holiday. Justin and Andrew were playing sports and making new friends. Life was good.

One summer, Justin and Andrew went to a local activity center during the day while I went to work. The director there organized a play called *The Lion King* (an urban version). Justin played Simba, the son of Mufasa and Sarabi. Andrew had a small speaking part, and he also danced in the play. I don't know how they knew about it, but a local television station reached out to us because they heard about this kid with one eye who was a good dancer. The play was a huge success. Justin did an interview for one of the local TV stations. Andrew and I were interviewed in the television studio of a major TV station and that was quite the experience.

I was so nervous, but Andrew was cool as a cucumber.

Life was falling into place for us and even though we had everything we needed, I kept noticing that on the rare occasions that I met Damien to exchange the boys, he was always driving a very expensive car or SUV and the boys were telling me about how their dad had hundreds of pairs of sneakers, nice watches, and this and that. I found this odd since he was only paying them $300 a month. He never gave a cent more, not for birthdays or holidays, not for sports, for anything that would cost him more than $300. In fact, when I once asked Damien for help after someone broke into our house twice and stole the boys' game console, sneakers, and other items, he told me to *"take it out of the $300,"* so I decided to subpoena his bank records. I almost fell out of my chair when I started to review those bank statements!

There were rows and rows of him living a very lavish lifestyle, with trips to San Francisco and other places, expensive restaurants known for great steaks, expensive jewelry stores, and department stores. Then I saw where all that money came from. He spent one year in Desert Storm in the USMC and had received 100% disability from the Veterans Administration with a back pay of over $100,000, meant specifically for taking care of him and his family, including Justin and Andrew. He received this windfall from both the VA and the Social Security Administration, but instead of helping them, he chose to keep it all for his new, immediate family, while receiving monthly disability payments of over $5,000 (tax free). He received more than $3,000 per month, tax free from the VA and more than $2,000 per month, tax free from the SSA. I was livid. I had picked a crook to be the father of my children.

I hired an attorney and took him back to court for child support modification and I won. Mimi even flew to Phoenix from Dallas to be one of my character witnesses.

His payments went from $300/month to $1200/month. Becky told me straight out that I would never see a dime of that money, so I put a lien on their house. They refused to pay the new court-ordered amount, resulting in a child support arrearage of more than $20,000 and when they sold their house, we got every dime of it.

Those years were challenging for sure. I was trying to raise two troubled boys on my own without any help from anyone. The legal fights regarding child support lasted for years. At one point, Becky gained full guardianship and conservatorship over Damien so that she could fight me directly in court over "*their*" money. Damien came into court in a wheelchair, looking like he had just taken a couple of muscle relaxers. It was truly pathetic to see the lengths that they would go to, trying to avoid paying Damien's fair share of child support.

The stress was affecting all three of us. I was doing my best to manage everything, but I wasn't super woman. Justin was a teenager, and he became rebellious. He was angry and resentful that he did not have his dad in his life. He blamed me for "*breaking up the family.*" He said that "*all men cheat*" and that I "*shouldn't have left.*" He started hanging around with the wrong crowd, skipping school and testing his boundaries. I took him to the juvenile detention center once to experience their "*Scared Straight*" program. I took him to counseling again, but he refused to participate (again). I did everything I could, but things got worse and ultimately, I made him go live with Damien, who at that time lived about an hour away. Becky did not like that arrangement at all.

A few months passed by when Damien told me that they were moving to Montana. From what I heard, a very angry man came to their home insisting that Damien stay away from his wife, so I gave Damien permission to take Justin with them.

I missed Justin terribly and he was mad at me for a long time. He didn't even call me on Mother's Day and that broke my heart. Justin graduated high school in Montana and then, according to Justin, Becky told Damien that he had to leave. He was working at a popular fast-food restaurant and Damien asked him how much money he made there. The next thing Justin knew, he came home from work one day and Damien told him that he had rented a studio apartment for him, and he knew that he could afford it, so his stuff was packed, and they kicked him out that day.

Later, when Justin and I worked things out, Andrew went to Montana to visit Damien and his brother Justin. The plan was that Justin would fly back home with Andrew to make sure he was safe, but when Damien dropped them off at the airport in Montana, after waiting some time, their flight got canceled due to inclement weather.

Justin tried to call Damien several times to pick them up from the airport, but he never answered. Eventually, Justin called Becky, but she could not get ahold of Damien either, so she picked up the boys and dropped them off at Justin's apartment. Justin and Andrew heard some noises coming from his apartment and when they walked in, they saw their dad, Damien, in a compromising position with a young Asian girl. But wait, that's not the best part. Damien proceeded to introduce Justin as his "*brother*" and Andrew as "*his brother's friend.*" You can't make this stuff up!

Many dead-beat dads have set the bar very low on fatherhood -- Damien buried it.

Andrew and Justin

Chapter Eleven: Clarity

It's amazing when you see yourself in your children. Developmental psychologists have found that children learn by imitating adults, particularly their parents, and I saw a lot of myself in both of my children - the good, the bad and the ugly. I was about 37 years old before I really started to take a long look at myself and take a deep dive into who I was and why?

I learned that children who are molested can experience profound and lasting effects in their development. It can also lead to the increased likelihood of depression, substance abuse, and difficulties in adult relationships. The effects of child sexual abuse can be devastating and impact the ability to form healthy relationships and cope with stress. I needed to understand these effects because now it was crucial for me to address them and to support my boys so that they would have a fighting chance at life.

For years, I felt guilt and shame, and I asked myself *why*? Why did I feel guilty when it wasn't my fault? I started to think that the guilt and shame I felt may have come from the parts of my body that felt good despite what was going on in my head. My mother had stimulated me sexually and awoken those thoughts and feelings in me whether I wanted them there or not. She had stripped away my innocence and I was very angry with her but still, she was my mom, and I had some compassion for her mental state, yet I couldn't help but wonder how much of it was under her control? She had always read those romance novels and talked to me about how romantic her encounter was with my biological father, so I even wondered if she was trying to recreate with me what she had with him, but does being mentally ill excuse her behavior?

I read somewhere that part of the healing process for sexual assault victims is to confront their abusers.

So, I remember trying to bring it up to her one day, hopefully in a way that would not trigger her into an episode, but all she did was rapidly shake her head "*No*" and then she shut down. I am sure that she must have remembered something, and I hated her for it.

I started making little changes that included being very self-aware of my negative thoughts and starting each day with positive affirmations and when my mind would go back to an unpleasant memory, I made a conscious effort to switch it to something good. I also prayed more, read my bible more, and I just knew that God was always with me.

On the rare occasion when I felt the itch to get out, I would go places solo. I was not looking for anything but just wanted to practice my social skills. I was feeling more confident, and it showed. It's funny how much attention you can attract when you're not on display. It just usually involved chatting it up with someone at a bar/restaurant/lounge; harmless and always led to "*I'm not dating right now*." However, one evening did not go as planned.

Ben came to visit me in Phoenix one year and we went to this nightclub. We were still friends, so as he was doing his thing, I sat at the bar chatting with the bartender when the bartender offered me a drink. My instincts are usually very strong, but that night was different. I took a few sips of my drink and then I started to feel weird. Everything was turning black, and I felt like I was fainting. Someway, somehow, I managed to make it to the ladies' room, where I went into the farthest stall and crouched down in the corner next to the toilet. The next thing I remember, someone was banging on the stall door yelling at me to "*Get out*!" The club was closed! I was in that stall the entire time! I checked myself everywhere and it did not appear that I had been touched, but I felt very foolish to have gotten myself in that predicament. I slowly crawled out of the bathroom stall and threw some water on my face. When I came out, Ben was standing there, and he was furious with me! He started yelling at me that he told me to "*Stop taking drinks from guys*!" and I told him that someone drugged me. All I could do was thank God for saving me, again.

I didn't go out for a long time after that. Then, one day at work, I was on a lunch break and reading a self-help book when this guy came up to me and said, *"Do you want to know my favorite self-help book?"* to which I answered, *"Sure."* He replied, *"How to get rich from writing self-help books."* I chuckled. I had decided not to date while the boys were younger but now that they were older, I thought that I might brush up on my flirting and dating skills while being a lot more cautious with my drinks.

I saw this man a couple of more times and each time he saw me, he would say *"Smile."* I guess I had a bit of a scowl on my face, and I liked that he reminded me to smile. Well, he finally got around to asking me out. This was going to be a new experience for me. His name was [William], and he was white and fine.

William and I developed a close friendship. I'm not sure why but I felt comfortable enough to share some personal things about myself with him. We both shared private information with each other. We came from two different planets, and I could see that he was shocked but intrigued. I was hesitant but curious. He was a great listener and when I told him about Damien and all the aggravation that I had endured, he asked me if I ever thought about being involved with a white guy. I am sure that my body language was saying *"Heck yeah"* but I just laughed nervously. I found that while William and I had different upbringings, with different music, foods, and cultures, somehow, we still connected and had a lot in common.

He taught me a lot of things, including the importance of creating budgets, credit scores and what affects them and how much it can affect your life. He was very complimentary and not just on looks. This *"stranger"* was making me truly see something in myself that I never saw before. He was financially secure and helped me out a lot. We went to fancy restaurants, and I even went with him to his fancy country club.

In private, he corrected my English, and I was grateful for that. He would say that I was so black and so white, and he loved everything about me. When I told him that I felt out of place at these predominately white functions, he taught me that I belonged anywhere that I was. It is fair to say that I even had some sexual breakthroughs with him. He taught me valuable lessons, and I was a happy student. He didn't just shower me with gifts, he was my friend, and he always listened to me, no matter what mood I was in. It was nice to have this *"Superman"* in my life. He made me feel safe and secure, but best of all, he adored me like no other man ever had.

He took care of my car, did my yard work and helped me with the house and pool. He helped me plan and finance vacations for the boys and me. It was kind of like a fairy tale, but not. I was not in love with him, but I wondered if I had ever truly been in love with anyone before when I didn't even love myself, but now, I was finally learning to do just that. I was turning into one of those happy people and that's when I first started to really see colors. I knew they existed but for most of my life, I was wrapped up in black and greys and that's all I could see but now all the colors of the world were highlighted for me, red, yellow, orange, *were these colors here the whole time*? They were beautiful and I could feel them. I felt full of love, life and hope, despite my challenges. I deserved to work hard for my happiness and over time, I started to understand that that type of self-love can only come from within no matter how many times people tell you to *"stay positive."* Those are wonderful reminders from people that I knew cared about me, but that fake smile wouldn't go away until I was ready to make it real.

William and I still dated on and off for a while, but I just wasn't ready to jump into another commitment. I was having too much fun exploring me.

I was enjoying dating and learning more about men too much to stop. It was surprising what some men will tell you when they realize that they won't be getting any. Some played the long game, but I was in control. I made the rules, and I set the tone. Always.

Sometimes, I would get caught up in the black and white thing. I was not envious of black guys dating white girls. I was just annoyed that they were putting black women down in the process, so one day, I decided to do a sort of *"Social Experiment."* I started dating another white guy. Let's call him [Chet]. Chet was also very handsome and fit. We enjoyed each other's company and spent a fair amount of time together. I was starting to get the hang of this interracial dating taboo and didn't mind a little private revenge. If these brothas wanted to see some white chocolate, I was going to show them some white chocolate.

I especially enjoyed going to soul food restaurants with Chet. I was tickled pink watching a whole slew of interracial couples (black guy/white girl) stare at us. Chet and I sat there giggling, while I ran my fingers through his silky blonde hair. It was a bonus when the waitress told us that we had *"good energy."* The look on most of the black guys' faces was something like '*I know she didn't*' or '*what brotha hurt her?*' and most of the white girls were busy looking at their man to make sure that he was not looking our way. It was awesome. Lol.

I was mostly just having fun, but it was unfair to any man, white or other, to lead him on into thinking that we had a future together. I knew that I had to break things off with him, but I really did not want to hurt him. Eventually, he made my task easier when I found women's lingerie in his gym bag. That was not the worse part - it turned out, the lingerie was his!

Half of Me

Chapter Twelve: Who's Your Daddy?

I love black men. Apparently, most women do. I really didn't want to experiment anymore. I was beginning to wonder if I was exploring white men in my attempt to understand my biological father, but what I really learned was that men are men because people are people.

I also felt that I had gained a peek into "*The Mans*" world and his overall outlook on life and his general opinion of the black race. William and I often debated political views. I'm ashamed to say this, but he taught me the term "*n-word rich*." I remember how I felt when I first heard him say it. First, I felt like punching him in the face, and secondly, I was embarrassed by what I knew that meant.

As I was developing this open outlook on life that allowed me to see these different perspectives with a dual lens, I realized just how dumb racism really is. The other aspect was that I still wanted to know who my real father was no matter what color he was.

My dad passed away early 2017 and I went back to Lawton for his funeral. It was a dreary rainy day. I sat in the first row at the funeral and Nikki got up to speak. She mostly talked about herself, including calling herself the matriarch of the family, when the matriarch (our mother) was still living and sitting in the front row. She thanked everyone for coming and then proceeded to mention the siblings and where they all had traveled from, which included a friend of hers, who she had claimed as her "*adopted*" sister, but she conveniently failed to mention my name. I said under my breath, "*Well, I guess I'm chopped liver.*" Her husband heard me and attempted to motion to her that she had forgotten me, then she abruptly paused her long, drawn-out speech and said to him, "*Huh?*" When he pointed at me, she simply replied, "*Oh yeah, Kaye.*"

She was never that bright. I skipped the repass and went right back to my hotel and took the next flight out. I only wish that I had said the proper goodbye to my mother that night.

At that point, Tom assumed power of attorney over our mother and handled all the finances, including paying the bills, and Nikki became medical power of attorney, making all of the medical decisions as they pertained to our mother.

Since my dad had passed away, I thought that would be my chance to actively seek out who my real father was and I made the mistake of mentioning it to Nikki, who was a daddy's girl. She deduced that since I no longer saw my dad as my dad, I therefore, didn't need any of *her* daddy's money. That figures because she was always a selfish, materialistic thief.

By that time, my parents owned three houses. Tom and Nikki sold each of them and kept the proceeds for themselves. Then, Nikki moved my mom to South Carolina to live with her. Nikki had not worked since the '80s so she had the time, space and means to hire caregivers for her. Then, I saw on social media that she had just purchased a huge upstairs house and paid cash for a Mercedes Benz. I could take a guess where she got all that money. She said that her husband got a huge raise. I didn't ask any more about it.

I would call my mom in South Carolina occasionally to see how she was doing and of course Nikki would always answer the phone. She often told me that my mom was asleep or busy and couldn't come to the phone and when I asked her how she was doing, she would say the same thing every time, "*as well as can be expected*" with no other details and dialog, seemingly rushing me off the phone. I was only concerned about her health, not her money.

One day, I got her on the phone, and I told her that I wanted to check on her and to let her know that the boys and I were doing fine. Towards the end of the conversation, I told her that I apologized for not calling as much and wanted her to know that even though she may not hear from me that often, that I loved and missed her. Then I heard a voice on the other end of the phone say, "*Awwww.*" It was Nikki listening in on the other end of the phone. I knew then that I would never be able to have a private conversation with my mother. And, just as I had suspected, Nikki continued to monitor the calls and make excuses for why my mother couldn't come to the phone. I knew that Nikki was only concerned about the money that my dad left my mom so, I called less.

I really felt betrayed by my mother for setting me up for failure even though she didn't know it (or did she?). I mean, I've never really felt like I fit in anywhere and I always found it difficult to trust anyone, particularly in intimate relationships. It's hard to describe to people who can just move on and get over their past trauma. That's great for them but for me, it was the uncertainty that was always looming in my mind, and I never felt quite complete, because people need to know who they are and where they came from. It wasn't just important to find my biological father to help me understand my paternal genetics, identify any inherited medical and psychological concerns, but just to explore that side of my family. As I thought more about it, I began to realize why it's important not to speak badly about your children's father. It was important to understand that children need to be able to love all of who they are, not just half of who they are and when negative things are said about the other parent, the child may internalize that if that parent is a bad person, then maybe they are too. It's no wonder I felt lost for so long. I had mental health on one side and the unknown on the other.

I was telling a friend one day about finding my biological father and he thought that he might have some connections to help me. I was excited and thought that it was a great idea. A few weeks later, he sent me an address, phone number and email address of a man with the same name as my biological father. He had been in the Army and stationed at Ft. Sill around the time of my conception. It sounded right, but I was afraid to reach out to him. I was afraid of rejection.

One Sunday morning, I emailed the person and gave a short summary explaining the reason for my email. Later that same day, I received a response email saying that I had "*the wrong guy.*" It went on to read that he was married in 1968 and sent to Vietnam that same year. I replied with a simple, "*Thank you.*" The funny thing was, a few months later, I received a response from the same email address, saying that he was, "*Sorry that it took so long to write back*" but that he was "*…not my father*" and he finished by wishing me well. I can only assume that it was his wife who initially responded.

I was disappointed, but I would not allow myself to be broken, so I took a break from researching. It wasn't until a few years later that I finally had my questions answered.

My Daddy and I

Chapter Thirteen: Soulmate

D o you believe in Soulmates? A person ideally suited just for you. Someone with whom you have a unique deep connection based on mutual understanding and acceptance. If you had asked me that question before I met my current husband, I would have said it was baloney.

Reconnecting with Cary was something that I never expected. I first met him years ago when we were both married. We both work in the legal profession and were introduced by a former mutual co-worker. He's a lawyer and I'm a paralegal. It's a small legal community, so I would see him at various legal functions around the city. We always briefly greeted each other but kept it respectful.

Now, years later, I saw him at a restaurant in uptown Phoenix, and we instantly remembered each other, then we exchanged numbers. It was 2018 in late September, when we had our first date. I knew this guy was special because he was an hour late for our first date and I waited for him. Had it been anyone else or at any other time, I would have left after 15 minutes. I just kept myself busy talking to other people.

We did the usual catching up and the conversation went smoothly. He was very easy-going, charming and very funny. Cary was under my usual 6' feet requirement and he was light skinned. He was handsome with beautiful green eyes and sexy bowed legs. I was never attracted to light-skinned men until I learned to love my own light skin. Cary fascinated me.

Cary swears to this day that he met me when I lived in Los Angeles. My friends and I used to go to *TGIF*, a then-popular bar and grill in Santa Monica, California, that was a cool place to hang out.

He says that he met me there and that I blew him off. I don't remember him, but he said that he used to wear Swatch watches and didn't wear the fashionable basketball shoes that were popular at the time. He said he probably wore his comfortable, run over, low-top Converse. I told him, *"that would explain it."* Since I've known Cary, he's always been that way, never trendy, he wears what he wants to wear (but he never looks out of sorts)!

We talked about our past relationships. He was married for about 7 years, and I was married for almost 10 years. We both learned a lot from those relationships and both of us decided that we never wanted to get married again. I mean, literally, we both wanted to make certain that the other person knew never to expect marriage. We had been there and done that. I asked him what he was doing that next week, and he said, *"I'm going to Brazil for my birthday."* It was his birthday at the beginning of October, and he had a guy's trip planned. Of course, I played it cool and was like, *"Oh, that sounds like fun."*

It was another couple of weeks before I saw Cary again. I remember that I missed him and that was unusual for me too, but I still wanted to hang on to my single life. I figured that I was tied down for almost 10 years and had not experienced certain things. I wasn't looking for any freak-offs, but I did want to explore a little. The next thing I knew, Cary and I were on a date and holding hands. I never knew that underneath this strong black man, who always appeared so serious was this sweet and kind man, with a heart of gold. I had no intention of getting into a relationship at that time, but fate had other plans.

We were getting close fast and it felt effortless. We went on vacations and had the best times that were full of laughter and fun. We were genuinely friends first and foremost and got along beautifully. The intimacy was natural, and I loved the way he held me. He made me laugh and feel safe and secure, but he came from a good family.

His parents and family were educated and loving. There was no dysfunction in his home. No yelling, no fighting, no drama, so I was careful not to scare him off.

Cary and I have a lot of fun together. He makes me laugh all the time and I love that, but he seems to think that I am the funny one (unintentionally). He loves teasing me about my Oklahoma upbringing. We talked about how lackluster education was in Oklahoma. When he asked me what foreign language I had to take in high school – the answer was "*none*." What I did learn, however, were the words to the song "*Oklahoma!*" from the famous musical. We had to sing it every morning, right after the Pledge of Allegiance.

One night, while we were out to eat, Cary and I ran into a judge that he knew. He introduced me to the judge, who was very nice, and when she asked me where I was from, my husband – for whatever reason – started telling the judge that I didn't have to take a foreign language in school, *BUT*, that I knew all the words to "*Oklahoma!*" He then turned to me and said, "*Ina, hit it!*"

Of course, I did *NOT* immediately launch into a full rendition of "*Oklahoma!*" I was mortified. Instead of singing, I asked my husband if he was crazy (which I believe he is – at least a little). The judge and her friend thought the whole exchange was funny, and we all had a good laugh!

Everything in me was telling me that this was the right decision, especially after I accidentally told him that I loved him first, which I always tried to avoid. I said it low because it really just slipped out one night. Then, he said, "*What?*" and I said, "*Never mind.*" Who was I kidding? My bad choices in men had just ended.

There were a couple of occasions that almost derailed us. He had some unfinished matters with a couple of females that he needed to handle first.

He was being nice, probably trying not to destroy his friendships with them just in case it didn't work out with me, but I was not having it. These chicks were not paying him any attention at all, then suddenly we start dating and they lose their minds. I found them to be extremely disrespectful to me and to our relationship, so I laid it out for him. I had taken too much crap from men in my life, and I wasn't about to take anymore -- "*handle these chicks, or I will.*" That's when he first met "*Kaye*" (my middle name). The girl from Oklahoma, who was "*about that life.*" I didn't want him to meet that version of me, but it was going to happen eventually. The second time Kaye came out was at an ASU vs. UofA football game (Cary is an ASU alumnus and life-long fan). Apparently, these two colleges are serious rivals. We're in the stands in Tucson (where the UofA is located), having fun and minding our own business. UofA was winning at the time, and a few fans were cheering their team on, albeit drunk and belligerent. We said nothing. Then, ASU took the lead, and we started cheering. These two white guys sitting behind us said to us, "*go back to Guadalupe!*" Before I knew, I turned around and said, "*we're black, dumbasses!*" Cary couldn't believe it! I forgot that I was trying to live the "*soft life*" but then, the guys really started talking crap (and loud), so I pulled out my cell phone and pretended to call someone. I said, "*Yea, it's me. We're at the game and these white boys are talking shit to us, telling us to go back to Guadalupe – oh okay, ya'll coming now? Cool, we'll be sitting right here in row (blah blah), aisle (blah blah) – okay, see you a minute.*" The whole time, Cary is in my other ear saying, "*I thought you didn't know anybody in Tucson.*" The next thing I knew, I turned around, and they were gone. Cary was shocked.

Another time, we were out to eat at a local soul food restaurant. Me in my secured shell and Mr. Friendly being nice to everybody. When our food came, there were some older, white ladies sitting in the booth near us.

One particular woman was so interested in the collard greens that she kept asking Cary, *"what's that?"* as she pointed to his plate. He said, *"which one?"* and she repeated her question again, as she pointed closer to his plate. He asked again, *"which one?"* and this time, she literally almost touched his greens and before I knew it, I slapped her hand away and said, *"don't touch his food!"* and he was so embarrassed. He just exclaimed (exasperated), *"Ina!"*

We were engaged five months later.

Light Skinned Love ❤️

Chapter Fourteen: Family

In 2019, I married Cary on my 50th birthday. It was a lovely wedding in Las Vegas. Everything was perfect and we had a great time, and this time, everything felt right. It was one of the happiest days of my life. Cary and I get along 99% of the time. The times when we disagreed mostly concerned my youngest son, Andrew. My older son Justin was still living in Montana but not doing that great, so we flew him back home to Arizona.

Justin adjusted to Cary just fine, but Andrew did not. They were too old to see Cary as a stepfather and I think they both continued to desperately long for a meaningful relationship with their own biological father.

After living with us for a while, Justin eventually got his own apartment. So, then it was just the three of us and our dogs but sometimes, there was tension just beneath the surface as it pertained to our blended family. Blended families suck. I think that because Andrew and I spent those last years just the two of us, he wasn't used to sharing my love and to him, Cary was just a guy that I brought home out of nowhere. He didn't realize that I had known Cary since the early 2000s and that he was far from a stranger, although I'm not sure that mattered much to Andrew.

Andrew was in high school and had made many friends, especially playing basketball and being awesome at it. Cary and I were always on the go in the beginning. We traveled to Palm Springs, Seattle, Mexico, Denver, and Tucson. We always stop at the same restaurant on our way back to Phoenix from Tucson. They make the most delicious bubble waffles!

It didn't really matter where we went, if we were together because we got along so well. That's when you feel in your heart that you are destined to be together. That it is fate, when you get along effortlessly and it's never awkward. We always laughed and had fun. I think that's what can happen when you start out as friends first, allowing yourself to be vulnerable, real and open, when liking the person seems more important than loving them because you truly enjoy them and it doesn't matter so much if they're not Mr. Olympia, because you are captivated by so much of their inner beauty.

I told Cary everything about me and he adored me nonetheless. He was raised in a wonderful family. You could say that he had an opposite upbringing than I did, but none of that mattered to him. Although he always encouraged me to let go of the past, he never discounted my pain. Up until that point, I was guarding my emotions with everything that I had, but it was something about Cary. In fact, as odd as it may sound, from the first moment that I met him, years and years ago, I felt like his name never left my mind. We were never involved before and really didn't know each other, to be candid, but there was something. I just couldn't put my finger on it, but his name just kept coming up throughout my life in one circle or another, and here he was 18 years later at the same restaurant and single this time!

I decided that Cary was the guy for me, and he became part of our family. I was introduced to many of his family members, and all but one of them made me feel more like family than I ever felt with my own so-called family. I was okay with being estranged from them because someone else *did* love me. He showed me that every day and I felt it all the time.

But Andrew started to rebel in the same way that Justin did at his age. I found myself in a familiar place, as a single black mom. I was trying to be understanding of yet another young black male, growing up without a male influence, angry and confused and in Andrew's case, he had a lot to be pissed off about, but it's a delicate balance being a single mother, to be both nurturing and the disciplinarian.

Andrew was being too disrespectful back then, and I wasn't having it, so after butting heads on a consistent basis, he decided that he wanted to go and live with his dad. The same dad that never called him just to see how he was doing. The same dad that denied him. The same dad that fought tooth and nail to avoid paying his fair share of child support to them. The same dad that never called them on their birthdays or holidays, and the same dad that attempted to smear their mother's name in open court and in court documents, so I felt betrayed by Andrew and let him go.

After less than a month, Andrew was calling me with his concerns. He finally understood that no one was going to love him like his mother. Damien was not picking him up from school. His so-called stepmother was buying fast food for herself and their children; while expecting Andrew to eat green bologna (he sent me the picture!). The last straw was when Andrew got really sick as has happened over many years (and continues to happen). I received an email from Becky, stating that she did not have time to deal with Andrew being sick because she had her own two children to raise. He was on the first plane smoking after that, and I welcomed him back with open arms.

I wished that my children had other family members to build relationships with, but I am all they have. No aunts/uncles, cousins, etc. and unbeknownst to me, they were about to lose their only remaining grandparent, even though she's someone who they barely knew.

It was in early 2022 when I was on social media just scrolling and reading the usual nonsense of the day when I received a direct message from a former neighbor in Lawton. She simply wrote, "*I'm sorry to hear about your mother.*" I was perplexed because no one had told me anything recently about my mom, so I asked, "*What do you mean?*" and she replied, "*She died.*" Gasp!

Yes, I had just learned through social media that my mother passed away. The two living so-called siblings, Tom and Nikki never said a word to me and cut me completely out of the will.

I knew that there would be issues when both of my parents passed away. I had seen so many families destroyed, both in my personal life and in my professional experience as a paralegal in estate planning matters, so I expected major drama, and I had long decided that I would never fight them over money or things left behind. They were both always greedy and selfish, so I decided to step back and let them fight it out.

I remember that after my father passed away, even after Nikki failed to mention me in my dad's eulogy, she had the nerve to call me and wanted to know if there was a way to find out if someone had an insurance policy. She said that our dad always had an insurance policy and that she believed that Tom had cashed in the policy as power of attorney, but instead, told her that as my dad was getting dementia towards the end of his life, he stopped paying the premiums on the policy, it supposedly lapsed according to Tom.

Nikki sent me screenshots of the bank statements showing personal charges made by Tom and/or his wife. It was at that time that I started doing a little investigation of my own and it appears that Tom and Nikki had created an LLC in their names only and were apparently paying themselves a salary for being our parents' caregivers, Tom, as power of attorney and Nikki, as medical power of attorney. They are truly a disgrace.

Once my mom was gone, Nikki told extended family that Tom had spent up all the money. Fortunately for me, I never counted on that money to begin with and unlike Nikki and Tom, I can still look in the mirror each day and know that I didn't lie, cheat and steal to obtain every dime of my parent's estate, while ignoring my parent's wishes as stated in their Will to split anything remaining.

Tom and Nikki are not my brother and sister. I hope to never see or hear from either of them again.

Chapter Fifteen: The Next Chapter

2024 was an interesting year indeed. After my dad passed away in 2017, I signed up with one of those DNA/genealogy companies and after I received my results, I was even more confused. The summary detailed a list of DNA information, including 39% DNA from England, Wales and Northwestern Europe, 19% Cameroon, Congo, and Southwestern Bantu, 14% Ireland and Scotland, 4% China, 2% Southeast Asia-Dai (Tai) and some Portuguese too, which only piqued my interest further.

From time to time, I received emails from this DNA company, informing me that they had found a match, usually a first, second or third cousin. The link from the company showed a breakdown of the DNA match, including whether it was from the maternal or paternal side. I was so excited every time I received these emails, and I quickly and eagerly opened them.

Many of the emails and messages that I received were from white people and it was always a delicate way that I tried to approach the fact that I was a biracial (black) woman looking for her white father. This information had to be disclosed eventually when I gave name, dates, and other information, so many of the conversations started out that way, but when I mentioned my black ancestry, I was left with an inbox full of ghosts. I mean really, how shocking must that be to find out that you might have a *"black"* relative, especially when you might not even *like* black people! When I stopped receiving responses, I understood and moved on.

I had almost given up hope and had stopped checking those emails and messages, then one day, I saw an interesting message from someone who identified herself as a potential second cousin.

The initial question was usually something like, '*How are we related?*' and then you share information with each other in the hopes of finding an answer and that's what we did.

After sharing names, places, and dates it turned out that my biological father was her grandfather's brother, and she knew quite a bit about him. The more I learned about him, the more questions I had. According to her, her immediate family was not around his side of the family a lot, so she asked some of her other family members about him, including one aunt, who had some accurate information and some not so accurate. I had to hear this person's voice because it did not feel real. Did this really just happen? After more than 50 plus years, am I really finding out who he is? I was in total shock and disbelief as my eyes filled with tears.

I called her and we talked for a long time, and she told me all the things she knew and had heard about him. Everything matched up and when I saw his picture, I knew that it was him. We have the same forehead and face shape. I cannot describe my feelings at that time, but I was relieved to finally have some answers and perhaps finally a piece of closure.

Unfortunately, my biological father passed away in 2018, so I would never have the opportunity to meet him. I was sad but tried to focus on the good. I read his obituary and saw that he had one surviving son; my half-brother named [Kyle]. He lives in Arkansas, and I reached out to him online. He too was in shock; almost speechless but never denied the possibility. I imagined that he started to conduct some due diligence of his own and eventually, we talked on the phone. It was incredible.

I had my guard up, expecting him and his family to reject me. He naturally had a lot of questions, and I was open and upfront. We must have talked for over an hour that first time, and I was pleasantly surprised that he was interested in getting to know me better and perhaps building a relationship.

For the next several months, we conversed by text message, just simple small talk here and there but a mutual effort to stay in touch, which pleased me. In just that short time, this guy was nicer to me than the people who called themselves my siblings and had grown up in the same house as me! He and his family even came to visit me in Phoenix, and I cannot begin to tell you how interesting that was as I looked in the face of a white man who shared my paternal DNA.

Over the next few months, the big hole that I always felt in my heart filled up with love and gratefulness. Again, take nothing away from my daddy who raised me like his own. He will always have a special place in my heart, and I love and miss him very much. I just needed to know the truth.

I am fortunate to still be in contact with two of my nephews, Evelyn's oldest son, [Lamont], and Tom's oldest son, [Chris], and some of my maternal aunts and cousins. After years of being away from my mom's family, we had a sort of family reunion in 2024. Cary and I visited them in Ft. Worth and had a wonderful time. It was like Thanksgiving in September with all the food and fixings. I felt so incredibly special that so many of my family on my mother's side traveled just to see me and we partied that whole weekend. I honestly did not know that they cared about me that much.

Today, I am in a much better place. I still get depressed sometimes, especially when it rains and when I allow myself to become completely overwhelmed by stress, but it doesn't last as long as it used to. I allow myself to cry and even scream into my pillow on occasion if I need to.

I give myself about 5 minutes to have a pity-party, but then I blow my nose, wash my face and stand tall again. I must be my own best friend sometimes and tell myself and believe that everything will be alright. I look around and see that things ain't so bad. At least, that's the mentality that I try to hold on to.

For instance, I was going through a lot a few years ago, when I was working in toxic environments. I left one job due to racial discrimination and walked into another job that was much worse. In the first job, I was told by the supervisor that I was lucky that the hiring manager offered me the job when she was out of the town, because she *"didn't hire people with funny names."* For some reason, I guess because of my lighter complexion, other races seemed comfortable openly discussing their disdain for black people, that is, until I made it clear where I stood. I even think that some black people may not believe that lighter skin black people can be subjected to racism, but it happens every day. At another job, I was bombarded with racially charged questions as if I was expected to answer on behalf of a whole race of people. They seemed confused that I identified as black when I could get so much more leverage mentioning my white heritage. They did not understand that I was proud to be black. A few people in that office openly referred to black people as *"Colored"* or *"Black Colored."* They were not quiet in their side conversations about race, religion and politics and anyone that did not share their views were ostracized and pressured to quit.

One day, I was sitting in my office minding my own business, when a secretary (Caucasian) yelled out to me saying, *"Well, I guess you'll be moving to California"* and when I said, *"Uh, no. Why?"* She then replied, *"Because they're giving their blacks reparations."* She was saying that she wanted to know *"where all that money was going to come from."*

This was someone who was not my friend and not friendly with me, who tried to sabotage my job by lying and deliberately omitting me from vital emails (again and again). She decided to blurt this out in front of everyone! This went on from 2019 to 2023. It increased my anxiety and depression and led to my low morale and poor productivity. I even started developing physical problems like stomachaches, headaches, and a rapid heartbeat. I was biting my tongue so much during the day that I was filled with anger by the time I got home. That is when I knew it was time to submit my letter of resignation.

I was falling into another deep depression during that time. It took a lot out of me to bite my tongue, endure the racism and take the disrespect. I felt like I had PTSD. I would get enraged just driving by the building. It was awful.

I wanted so badly to understand my depression and why I couldn't just "*snap out of it.*" I used to have a friend who was a psychologist and he explained it this way:

> Imagine your mind filled with different rooms. There's a room of happiness, sadness, anger, etc. Everyone gets sad, right? They walk into their room of sadness and after a short while, they say to themselves, "*this room sucks. I'm getting out of here!*" and they promptly feel better but if you have a chemical imbalance, that is likely inherited, when you try to open the door with your key to get out of the "*sad room,*" your key slips and you can't get out.

It was sad when I first started my current job, because I used to be on edge all the time. I knew that I had racial fatigue and that resulted in symptoms similar to post-traumatic stress disorder. Over time, those feelings slowly subsided. I now have a job that I love.

My boss is awesome, and my coworkers are cool. I just had to be patient and wait for the right fit. Another blessing right on time.

So, yes, I still get depressed from time to time. In fact, I was just feeling really depressed the other week and that lasted for about four days. I'm extremely concerned about my sons in this current hostile environment and when it consumes me, it takes everything I have to stay still and trust that God has the final say and occasionally, I still see that little girl, hurting and lost, but I remind her to stay strong.

I understand now how important it is to have a support system. I didn't have that, but enough people played enough integral roles throughout my life, that their support always reminded me to be strong and remain steadfast in my trust in the Lord. It has always been God's timing (the perfect timing). For each of those wonderful people, I am grateful.

Ultimately, you owe it to yourself to find your own version of mind over matter. Taming your anxiety and depression triggers start with knowing what activates you and throws you off balance. When I get sad sometimes, I love that Cary tries to cheer me up or make me get out of the house, but getting out of bed and pushing past the negative stuff is the work that I must do. Today, I know that I'm worth it.

I know that no matter what comes my way, my faith sustains me, and God did not give me the spirit of fear, so I will continue to rise and persevere through every black cloud that tries to darken my path. It's not just the power of positive thinking, it is the power of the tongue with faith, to speak only good things in your life and fight against all negative thoughts, the sincere belief that you know, that you *know*, God is real.

As for Andrew and Justin, they're adults now. Andrew aspires to be a successful rap artist, and Justin is working in corporate America with plans to go back to college. I am proud of the men that they are becoming.

Looking back on my life now, the one thing that I would do differently is worry a lot less. You could say that we all live between our ears and face the dreaded battle of the mind, but the strongest force is the one that *you* feed.

I pray that each of you keep fighting for your own happiness and that you find peace in your heart, mind, and soul despite the ugly things that may have had you believing that you would be better off unalive. I am here to tell you that you are not better off! Please find something to love about yourself. There is something beautiful about every person. Believe in yourself and never let anyone steal your joy! I'm not special and if I can do it, you can too! If you think you can't do it by yourself, I encourage you to seek the Lord and pray for wisdom, healing, and guidance and remember to **Smile! You got this!** 😊

Me – Happy

Epilogue/Conclusion

As one slowly loses hope in life and in themselves, it can be a hard and lonely road to navigate. You feel broken, helpless, lost and afraid. When life overwhelms you, please pause and take a deep breath and remember that all of your pain in life builds muscle. It can bring out your strength, or it could break you. The decision is up to you and the strength to persevere is within you. You must believe it. Remember, *YOU ARE NOT ALONE!*

It is also important to unload and unburden yourself of past trauma. You will not be able to ignore it forever, and the last thing you want it to do is allow it to manifest itself physically. You must face your challenges head on and then move past them, even if that means confronting people who hurt you. If you don't want to go to a professional counselor or psychologist, please find someone that you can <u>trust</u> and tell them what happened to you. Allow them to share something with you. Get it out some way or another, whether in writing, journaling, music, art or other expressions. Face it, fight through it and move on to find a healthier you. Let's shine a light on the stigma of mental illness, because, yes, mental health matters.

And lastly, please don't worry about judgment from other people. When someone says to me, *"Oh, I'm not judging you."* I nicely reply, *"I know that you are not. You don't have the authority to judge me."* People may think that they are judging you, but they are merely voicing their opinion. Stop caring about what people think. It's much more important to care about what you think of yourself.

Life is too short and precious to waste so make every heartbeat count.

Acknowledgments

I want to first thank God. He has watched over me and protected me for a long time and I would not be writing this book if it were not for His grace and mercy. This is my testimony.

Thank you to my children, [Justin] and [Andrew]. You were there for me when we only had each other and through all our ups and downs, and my emotional mood swings, you always loved me no matter what. I never experienced real love until I had my babies and I thank you both for giving me a reason to live.

Thanks to my wonderful husband, Cary for inspiring me, loving me, believing in me, and putting up with me while I wrote my story. The process had my emotions like windshield wipers, but you always encouraged me to keep going. I appreciate you so much.

I love and adore you all more than you'll ever know.

About the Author

Ina is a mother and wife currently residing in Phoenix, Arizona with her sons and husband. She is also the "dog mom" to her beloved Chihuahua-Pomeranian mix, "Cookie."

She is a paralegal and writer who has been working in the legal field for over 30 years. Ina loves to travel, especially to beach destinations. She enjoys spa days, listening to live music – especially smooth jazz, hiking, bird watching, and just about anything else relaxing.

www.ingramcontent.com/pod-product-compliance
Lightning Source LLC
Chambersburg PA
CBHW060626130626
46555CB00002B/681